Tend Your Own Garden First

by

Nancy Eichman

IBSN: 0-89137-457-4

Dedication

—To my parents Cecil and Milbra Chaffin
who first lovingly planted the Seed in my heart

—To my husband Phil
who patiently waters

—To my God
who graciously gives the increase

Bouquet of Roses and Many Thanks To...

—To Jane McWhorter
for her assistance and encouragement to keep with it

—To Betty Watson
for her time and invaluable comments

—To my husband Phil
for his patience and editorial help

—To my children John and Amy
for inspiring me to write this book

Table of Contents

Confessions of a Purple Thumber

It does not surprise me (or anyone who knows me) that I have not received the Green Thumb Award. The local Garden Club has not bestowed on me their coveted Golden Rose, nor have I walked away from the County Fair with a blue ribbon in the gardening division. I must confess that there is a good reason. Plants cringe when unfortunate enough to be in my care. Singing does not help—my melodies are funeral dirges to them. I overwater cacti, underwater ferns, water spray African violets and hoe the garden with a fervor that leaves both weed and vegetable slaughtered in my path. Survival of the fittest is the rule when under my supervision. Only the strong survive!

So it probably will amaze my friends (and especially my husband!) that I would attempt to write a book having anything to do with gardens. But I speak of a spiritual garden of tender hearts with eternal Seed to sow. Let me explain how this book took root.

Every Wednesday night after Bible Study, our kindergartener John would bring home a different card with a book of the Bible written on it. The cards were nothing fancy, just cardboard with the book written in crayon. One night I was amazed at how many books of the Bible he knew by memory. I was surprised because we had not drilled him very much at home so his practice came mostly from Bible School. I was curious to know what type of nifty visual aid or unusual memorization technique the teacher was using to teach these rather difficult names.

When I took a peek in the classroom, I found no expensive store-bought list, but rather the same type of cards that John had been bringing home. The cards were put in rows and had the books of the Bible in crayon. The children just repeated the books week after week. I thought, "I could do THAT at home! My next thought was, "Why haven't I done that more!"

Are you like me? We roll glibly along, thinking our children are learning God's Word through osmosis. We believe we are teaching our children the Bible at home and perhaps we are. But like me, we can all probably do better. We think we are doing an adequate job but is "adequate" enough? Do we expect Bible School teachers to fill in the gaps? How big are those gaps?

The purpose in writing this book is to aid us as parents in improving the quality and variety of our Bible teaching at home. It is my search for practical ideas to make the Word an exciting guidebook for living for my two children. It is not a "miracle manual" in which every idea works, but rather a "working manual" still in process. This book was not written to raise our level of guilt. Rather, I hope it will raise our consciousness of what, where, when, and especially how we can teach and train our children about God's revelation to man. There are so many possibilities. Let us not limit them.

Bible school teachers or even Christian school teachers do not have the same opportunities we have at home. WE must take an active part in teaching our children God's Word. God has given us as parents the responsibility of tending our spiritual gardens and they are waiting to be tilled. If this book helps in some small way to encourage you to teach the Bible to your children, then my prayer will be fulfilled.

A Parable

"...my own vineyard have I neglected."
(Song of Solomon 1:6)

Once in a kingdom not so far away in a time not so long ago there was a poor farmer who owned a small plot of land. Besides the ramshackle hut where he lived, he had nothing much else he could call his own. His pride and joy was his garden—it meant everything to him. This spring, as he did every spring, he set out to till the clumps of hard earth. As he worked the soil, the rich earth churned under his dilapidated old plow. When planting time was near, he traveled many miles to the village to pick up the King's precious seed to plant. Upon returning, he was eager to start sowing.

Laden with his seedbag, he dug down and carefully placed each seed in its place. Then he covered it gently with his hands. He made sure each seed was planted the precise depth and distance from each other. With loving care, he watered the garden and anxiously awaited the first sign of life.

Then they appeared—the first shoots! The farmer weeded and watered, weeded and watered. This was to be his best garden yet!

The King rode by one day and noticed the farmer's fine garden. The farmer's careful attention to his garden was evident. The healthy, tender sprouts in arrow-straight rows impressed the King and he praised the farmer.

"You are to be commended for your beautiful garden," exclaimed the King. "The best of all the crops in the land will be brought to the Great Harvest Homecoming. I hope to see you and your bounty there."

Then off the King rode, spreading the news of the grand event for which only the best of the crops would do.

The humble farmer was thrilled that the King would even notice his small plot. The villagers were impressed too. They wanted him to share his successful techniques of planting and growing so their gardens would also be the objects of such praise. So they began to make plans for the farmer to share his knowledge in seminars and speeches.

At first the farmer found it hard to leave his garden so much. After all, it was like a CHILD to him. But in his "busyness," his garden was soon forgotten.

One of the King's servants made frequent trips to this village and he noticed that the farmer's garden, though growing, was showing signs of neglect. He called this to the farmer's attention.

"Farmer, it seems the carrots need thinning and the tomatoes need stakes. Shouldn't you take time out from your busy schedule and do these things?" the servant asked.

"Oh yes, but I have to give my speech to the PTA (Peasants and Tradesmen Association). It's called, 'Raisin' 'Em Right.' Nifty title, huh? Anyway, I can tend to that tonight. I'm setting aside five minutes of QUALITY TIME every evening before bedtime to take a look at my garden. Isn't that great! After all, it's QUALITY TIME instead of QUANTITY TIME that matters."

As the farmer rushed away, the servant wondered two things: (1) How the farmer could see his garden well in the dark (even with a torch) and (2) How such a small QUANTITY of time could be sufficient for QUALITY time.

It was true that the Plant Teacher came by twice a week. Complete with the latest visual aids, he would encourage growth by teaching lessons about the Master Gardener. But there was only so much he could do. After all, he only came twice a week and the garden needed daily attention.

It seemed a blight was overtaking some of the vegetables in the little garden. The servant caught the farmer at home once and told him.

"Oh, is that right?" exclaimed the farmer. "We must do something about that. Let's see. . .how about the Young Sprout Director? Why couldn't he come and take care of that? ISN'T THAT WHAT HE'S PAID FOR? Anyway, the plants would probably do better if they had more entertaining, stimulating activities to stretch their horizons. I mean, after all, how much fun is it to just GROW? Could you take care of that? I've got to get on to my speech 'Gardening Around the Castle' to the Castle Builders."

The Young Sprout Director did come but it seemed the garden was not interested in growing or in entertaining, stimulating activities. He relayed this to the farmer.

On hearing this news, the farmer hurriedly said, "I'm late for my 'Sowing Seminar.' How about the Plant Preacher? Haven't I read in the latest research bulletins that talking to plants is good for them? Why doesn't he come and talk to them? After all, ISN'T THAT WHAT HE'S PAID FOR?"

The Plant Preacher did come and talk to the plants. But since they had not been spoken to much before, the experience was a strange one to them and was not very effective.

The Plant Preacher told the servant of his concern for the garden. They urged the farmer to see how the garden was being destroyed by insects and how it was shriveling up from lack of water and nutrients. Their warning reached dull ears.

"I can't go to work in the garden now. After I finish my 'Reaping Revival' tonight, I'm heading straight for my vacation. I've worked hard and I deserve it. But I know what I'll do! I'll send the garden to S.O.I.L. University. I hear they can do marvelous things for situations like this." And grabbing his vacation gear, the farmer was gone.

At S.O.I.L. University the warmth and goodness of the atmosphere made plants flourish even when the soil was not always the best. But alas, it was too late for the implanted seeds of the farmer's garden to grow well. The plants were clearly dying. The soil was sent home, along with the great bags of fertilizer and gardening tools. The fertilizer was barely opened and the tools were never used.

One day not long after that, the King was surveying the fields of the village. The luscious vegetables hung plump and juicy from their vines. The branches of the fruit trees were heavily laden from the weight of their bounty. The King smiled with anticipation. The Harvest Homecoming would be grand indeed.

He eagerly stopped at the garden of the farmer who had helped the other villagers with their crops. "His garden will be a sight to behold," the King thought to himself.

It was indeed a sight to behold. The gate swung open and to his horror the King saw decaying fruits and vegetables. The air reeked with the stench of rotten tomatoes and spoiled squash. Some plants had died before they had the chance to produce and lay withered on the earth. Weeds had overtaken others. The once airy fragrant blossoms of the apple and pear trees had produced fruit that was stunted and sour. Insects had finished off the rest. What a sparse and sickly harvest! What a meager, shrunken, shriveled sight!

Upon this scene came the farmer just as he was returning from his extended vacation. His face filled with disbelief, first when he saw the garden, but more so when he saw the King.

"Where is the harvest?" demanded the King.

"I. . .eh. . .don't know. I know I started the garden ever so carefully. I then put it in the hands of those others while I was away. Let's see—there was the Plant Teacher, the Young Sprout Director, the Plant Preacher and S.O.I.L. University. Couldn't they do any better than that?" the farmer hedged.

The King ordered his soldiers, "Throw this farmer in the burning garbage pit with his decomposed fruits and vegetables." As the farmer was led away, the King sadly spoke. "I demanded no more than you could do. But you have betrayed my trust and confidence. I gave you the precious seed and now it is as good as lost. Your garden plot was yours to care for. Your responsibility was first to that land. Although the other gardens are just as important to me, you must TEND YOUR OWN GARDEN FIRST!"

CHAPTER ONE

How Does Your Garden Grow?

"...you are God's field..." (I Corinthians 3:9)

I am not a gardener. I am afraid my thumb is purple rather than green. If it were not for my husband, the biologist, our house would be graced with shriveled brown plants in varying degrees of death. Some plants wilt when they see me coming. They reason, "Why wait for a slow lingering extinction. We'll just get it over with!" Some people pay someone else to house-sit for their plants while they are gone. They pay me to stay away!

Yet in another sense God has made me a gardener. When our children were born, God made my husband and me accountable for physically clothing and feeding them. But more importantly, we were blessed with the impressionable soil of their young hearts. We have a great impact on what will spiritually bloom from that rich soil.

Every parent has in his care a spiritual garden with its blessings and responsibilities. Our responsibility does not stop with our children, but it certainly starts there. The whole world is "ripe for harvest" (John 4:35). We should do what we can to care for the needs of this world, but in doing so we must not neglect our children's spiritual well-being.

JESUS' USE OF GARDENING TERMS IN HIS PARABLES

Jesus used the concepts of sowing, reaping, and harvesting frequently in His parables. Palestine at that time was principally an agricultural region and the common man was linked to the soil for his livelihood. The crowds might have been able to look out and see the reapers harvesting when he spoke, "The harvest is plentiful but the workers are few" (Matthew 9:37). Or perhaps they saw weeds growing among the crops when He taught about the tares being sown by the enemy (Matthew 13:24-30,36-43). Possibly they were shaded by the mustard tree's far-reaching branches but remembered its tiny beginning (Matthew 13:31-32). They

1

probably wondered, like the farmer in Jesus' parable, how life could spring from a dead-looking seed (Mark 4:26-29). And they might have seen a sower spreading seed in the field when Jesus began, "The sower went forth to sow his seed. . ." (Luke 8:4-15 ASV).

In the Parable of the Sower, Jesus contrasts four unique types of soil. These soils represent different kinds of hearts of man. The seed sown is the Word of God.

Some seed sown by the wayside was trodden under foot and devoured by the birds. This soil illustrates a heart so hardened and insensitive that the Word cannot penetrate it. Satan comes and snatches the Seed away.

The seed that fell on rocky places sprang up but took no root. When the sun came out and scorched the tender plant, it withered away. The impulsive, shallow heart joyfully receives the Word and endures for a while, but eventually stumbles in persecution.

Some seed landed among the thorns. After a while the seedlings were choked out and bore no fruit. The heart shown by this soil was initially receptive to God's Word, but was soon choked by the cares and riches of the world.

The seed also fell on good ground and yielded fruit thirty-fold, sixty-fold and a hundred-fold. The good, honest heart illustrated here was one who hears, accepts and obeys God's Word.

In surveying the various types of soil, we hope and pray that our families will have the receptive hearts who heed and obey. But how does our garden grow now?

Perhaps we initially received the Word in gladness and obedience but are we constantly feeding our soil with the nutrients that it truly needs? Have our hearts become hardened or shallow? Are we choking God's Word out of our lives with clubs, sports and even the "busyness" of church work? What fruit are we producing? How about our children?

"BY THEIR FRUITS YOU SHALL KNOW THEM. . ."

It is encouraging to see some of the fruit that is being produced in the Lord's church. Some congregations have increased their contribution and are growing numerically. Missionaries are thoroughly preparing themselves in teams to multiply their efforts in foreign fields. New outreaches are being implemented for the poor, handicapped, elderly and youth.

But other things are disturbing.

1. Our preaching has often become watered down. We used to know Scripture by heart because we heard it from the pulpit so often. Will our children have the same advantage?

2. Our Bible study classes are often showcases for our lack of study and knowledge of God's Word. Some classes are no more than a short Bible story and non-related games for the young and therapy sessions or guilt trips for the older. In one adult class the teacher said that the mandrake in Genesis 30:14 was a male duck! The

truly sad thing was that only a few members in the class knew any differently. Not only had the teacher failed in his study—the class was guilty too! Are we sometimes babes in "Spiritual Pampers" that the writer in Hebrews speaks of:

In fact, though by this time you ought to be teachers, you need someone to teach you the elementary truths of God's word all over again. You need milk, not solid food! Anyone who lives on milk, being still an infant, is not acquainted with the teaching about righteousness. But solid food is for the mature, who by constant use have trained themselves to distinguish good from evil (Hebrews 5:12-14).

3. Some of our congregations have "dill pickle" worship. They are PRESERVING the tradition with a sour monotony, and not RESTORING the vim and vitality of worship that must have characterized the New Testament church.

Some worship services have become routine at best and banal at worst. Out of more than 700 songs in our hymnals we choose to sing the same 50-100 the most often. At times our prayers are trite. We go through the motions of worshipping God with our lips but our hearts are far from Him (Mark 7:6).

4. Our families are in a state of flux. So many different units make up a family these days that we search for terms to define them—"nontraditional," "reconstituted," and "blended." (Sounds more like orange juice than people!) The most evident sign of this breakup is divorce.

Society is breeding a fragmented family by its frenzied pace and demanding schedules. Appointments, club meetings, luncheons, cultural affairs, sports activities, and friends—all demand our attention. Even church leaders fall into this "busyness" trap by not making time for their families. What results is a family which does not spend much time together and does not have a lot in common, except its heredity and address. Some homes are like gas stations—we fill 'em up, hand over the cash or credit card, and they are ready to go!

5. Our brotherhood is divided. This is certainly nothing new. Whenever two brothers or sisters are gathered together, there is the possibility of division. But the splintering of churches in communities across the nation and world is disheartening. Many times the matter in question is one of strength of personality or of opinion. And so the backbiting and discord go on.

6. We are losing our children for the Lord. We are not losing all but we are losing many. The tot whose enthusiasm burns with "This Little Christian Light of Mine" becomes the adult whose fire is all but extinguished. If the church would baptize and keep its own children faithful, it would grow at a rate of 25 percent in 10 years.[1]

WHAT'S A PARENT TO DO?

Surely the solutions are not simple, but clearly one thread runs through these

3

problems. WE LACK THE SPIRITUAL MATURITY that comes through BIBLE STUDY and ITS APPLICATION TO OUR LIVES. Could God say of us as He did of the children of Israel, ". . .my people are destroyed from lack of knowledge. . ." (Hosea 4:6)?

Knowledge of God can only come through study. There is no substitute for reading and studying God's Word for ourselves and then teaching our children. We would not let our children go naked in the snow or starve on only a meal a week. But spiritually we are not doing much better than that. Man cannot live by bread alone (Deuteronomy 8:3). We must feed and clothe our spiritual selves with God's Word to be prepared for the spiritual droughts and blizzards ahead.

Whether you are married, divorced, separated or single; whether you are rich or poor or middle-class; whether your mate is a Christian or not; if you have children, teaching the Bible begins in your home. We each have a garden to tend.

Say, how does your garden grow?

CHAPTER 1
HOW DOES YOUR GARDEN GROW?
Digging Deeper

1. Why did the people at that time understand Jesus' references to agriculture?

2. Examine Jesus' parables about sowing, reaping, and harvest to see how they fit into the context of His teaching.

3. After examining the Parable of the Sower, explain how these people exemplify the different types of soil: the Pharisees, the rich young ruler, Judas, Ananias and Sapphira, Paul, Cornelius, Simon the Sorceror, John Mark.

4. How do thoroughly prepared, Bible-based sermons stimulate spirituality in the local congregation?

5. How does lack of spiritual growth show itself in the Bible school classroom?

6. What is the context of Hebrews 5:12-14, in which the writer accuses his listeners of still needing someone to teach them?

7. Explain the term "dill pickle worship" in the church.

8. How can God's Word help make "peanut butter families"—families that stick together whether the way is smooth or crunchy?

9. In the church, how do we tell the difference between divisions based on biblical reasons and those based on opinion?

10. Give reasons why you think the church is losing many of its young people.

CHAPTER TWO

But I Don't Have a Green Thumb!

"Do not be deceived: God cannot be mocked. A man reaps what he sows. The one who sows to please his sinful nature, from that nature will reap destruction; the one who sows to please the Spirit, from the Spirit will reap eternal life." (Galatians 6:7-8)

Inadequate gardeners, like myself, are quick to think of excuses to explain our failures on the "green scene." It might be a failure to water correctly or fertilize adequately or plant the seed properly. But when it comes down to the nitty gritty, blaming the "purple thumb" sounds like as good an excuse as any!

"Ifs...ands...buts." The Lord has heard these words many times throughout history. Excuses abound in mankind's vocabulary. Moses stammered, "BUT, behold, they will not believe me..." and "BUT I am slow of speech..." (Genesis 4:4,10 KJV). Gideon hesitantly countered, "IF thou wilt save Israel by mine hand, as thou hast said..." (Judges 6:36 KJV). One who offered to follow Jesus said, "...BUT let me first go bid them farewell, which are at home at my house." (Luke 9:61 KJV).

So it is no surprise that we might offer the Lord a few excuses about tending our own gardens—teaching our children. Let us look at some of these excuses.

"I DON'T HAVE A TEACHING DEGREE. I didn't major in education. I didn't even go to college. I don't know all the methods and theories of teaching. I just couldn't do a sufficient job."

John Holt, proponent of the home schooling movement, aptly wrote:

...Human beings have been sharing information and skills, and passing along to their children whatever they knew... Along the way they have built some very complicated and highly skilled societies. During all those years

5

*there were very few teachers in the sense of people whose only work was teaching others what they knew. And until very recently there were no people at all who were trained in teaching, **as such**. People always understood, sensibly enough, that before you could teach something you had to know it yourself. But only very recently did human beings get the extraordinary notion that in order to be able to teach what you knew you had to spend years being taught how to teach.[1]*

Holt's point is well taken. If you know something or know how to do something, you can usually teach it to someone else. If we know God's Word and apply it in our lives, then the teaching will get done and the methods and theories will not be so important.

Perhaps the Lord could say to us as he did to Moses, "Now go, I will help you speak and will teach you what to say" (Exodus 4:12).

"I CAN'T AFFORD TO TEACH MY CHILDREN. I can't buy a bunch of Bible dictionaries and concordances. Have you seen the price of those sets of commentaries?"

Fortunately, the Lord did not command that we buy every known Bible study aid. He said to teach the Word. In a later chapter we will discuss various aids that might be helpful and ways to teach the Bible using something everyone has— "imaginality." But what the Lord requires is a Bible in hand and a willing heart to teach.

Actually, we cannot afford NOT to teach our children. Their souls' salvation— and ours—depend on it.

"I DON'T HAVE ENOUGH ENERGY. I work hard. You expect me to plan lessons and teach creatively while my eyelids are being held open with toothpicks?"

God answered Moses' feeble plea of slow speech with "Who made your mouth?" To us deadheads at the end of the day, he could ask, "Who made your body?" If we say we are too tired after we have attended, hosted, and coordinated every other activity, then our children are not getting our best. They and the Lord are getting the crumbs of our energy.

Instead, why not plan our days to take advantage of our peak energy times? And why not set aside some Bible time for our kids?

"I DON'T HAVE ENOUGH TIME. Do you really know my schedule? Between working, cleaning, cooking, I don't even have time for myself, much less the Lord."

We might have different amounts of education, money, or energy but we have the same of one thing—time. The whole point is that some people make better use of their time than others. The Christian's concern is to spend his time on things that count for an eternity rather than on things that will pass away. The "Busy Martha" complex wars against the "Listening Mary" complex. Mary chose the better part and so should we.

6

Let us get practical. Do you, right now, have a set time for reading and meditating on God's Word? Do you have a general time? (Between waking up and going to bed is TOO general!) Think about your day and whittle 15 minutes out of it to begin that time. Have you made the time to teach your children? Think up ways to chisel out time for your own life and schedule. After all, it is not our time—it belongs to the Lord.

"I DON'T KNOW ENOUGH ABOUT GOD'S WORD. After all, I didn't go to a Christian school or college. I've just been a Christian a few years."

This might be true, but ignorance is not excusable. Our lack of knowledge will not pardon us from teaching our children. Growing in the grace and knowledge of God's Word is something that we can all do—whether simple, smart, or any shade in between! It can be done but it will take dedication and determination on our part. The Lord will help us learn so that we may teach.

Look back at our excuses. Can you imagine all the dedicated Jewish mothers and fathers throughout history looking at our excuses with disbelief? Lack of teaching degrees, money, energy, time, or knowledge were not their principle concerns. They were commanded to teach their children and they did so the best they could. That is all that God expects of us.

THE RIGHT AND WRONG MOTIVES

We must have the right motives in teaching our offspring. Mary White, in her excellent book GROWING TOGETHER, points out five ways that negative motivation by itself can lead to dreary times for all concerned.

1. *GUILT—"The preacher said we HAVE to have family devos."*
2. *REGRET—"We've already wasted 15 years with our kids. Guess it's now or never."*
3. *LEGALISM—"If we don't do it, we'll go to hell."*
4. *DESPERATION—"Our kids are going wild—we've got to do something!"*
5. *AUTHORITARIANISM—"My children are going to listen to these Bible stories whether they like it or not."*[2]

Clearly, the parent with these attitudes will be as miserable as the child he teaches! But what are some of the right reasons?

WE ARE COMMANDED TO TEACH OUR CHILDREN GOD'S WORD

Scripture makes it plain that God not only desires but commands parents to teach their children.

"Fathers, do not exasperate your children; instead, bring them up in the training and instruction of the Lord" (Ephesians 6:4).

"The fear of the Lord is the beginning of knowledge: but fools despise wisdom and discipline. Listen, my son, to your father's instruction and do not forsake your mother's teaching" (Proverbs 1:7-8).

"My son, keep your father's commands and do not forsake your mother's teaching. Bind them upon your heart forever; fasten them around your neck. When you walk, they will guide you; when you sleep, they will watch over you; when you awake, they shall speak to you. For these commands are a lamp, this teaching is a light, and the corrections of discipline are the way to life" (Proverbs 6:20-23).

In verse 22 above, do you see the great influence for good the Scriptures can have on our children? When they go out in the world, the Bible can lead them. When they sleep, God's Word can give them peace of mind. When they awaken, the Scriptures can speak to them or be on their minds. Would we want anything less for our kids?

WE WILL BE JUDGED BY IT. We usually do not knowingly let our children go to school unprepared without their homework. We realize they will be tested and grades will be given according to their work. Yet at the final judgment, grades will be based on God's Word, the greatest textbook, and the grades will be either PASS or FAIL. What will be the result if we do not even know the words we or our children will be judged by?

Jesus said, "There is a judge for the one who rejects me and does not accept my words; that very word which I spoke will condemn him at the last day" (John 12:48).

OUR SOUL SALVATION DEPENDS ON IT. James wrote, ". . .humbly accept the word planted in you, which can save you" (James 1:21). "Save" here means not only to be forgiven from past sins but "to keep safe; preserve." The implanted Word saves us and keeps saving us from a habitual life of sin. It can keep us pure and holy.[3] The Psalmist said, "I have hidden your word in my heart that I might not sin against you" (Psalms 119:11).

WE MUST SHARE THE SEED WITH OTHERS TO PROPOGATE THE SEED. How dynamic is our influence to reach a lost world when we are not reaching our own in the church? How can we share the Good News with others when we have not even told our families? By teaching and converting our children first, we could then multiply our manpower, enthusiasm and influence to bring others to Christ.

THE BIBLE WILL GIVE US ANSWERS TO LIFE'S QUESTIONS. Peter affirmed to Jesus, "Lord, to whom shall we go? You have the words of eternal life" (John 6:68). The Bible holds the answers to mankind's resounding questions like: Who am I? What am I doing here? and Where am I going? How much better for our children to discover God's answers than those of some pagan philosopher!

8

GOD'S WORD CAN PREPARE US FOR TEMPTATION. The devil misquoted God's words when enticing Eve with the luscious fruit in the Garden of Eden. Satan misquoted Scripture when he tested Jesus in the wilderness. He has been twisting the words of the Bible to meet his purposes ever since. Christ overcame the devil's fiery darts by hurling Scripture back at him. What a great defense for temptation in our own lives!

THE BIBLE EQUIPS US FOR LIFE'S PROBLEMS. The Christian life is the best and the happiest life. But problems will come. When they hit, we are assured that God is not taking a vacation. He will not even be taking a catnap! (Psalms 121:3). The solutions may not be simple but God's Word can give us the help we need to find answers. Especially are Psalms, Proverbs, and Ecclesiastes chocked full of advice to help us avoid circumstances that can lead to trouble. We will be better prepared to avoid a problem than having to unscramble an existing one.

IF WE WAIT, OTHER PHILOSOPHERS WILL CONVERT OUR CHILDREN. Every person believes in something. Everyone has a god whether it be Buddha, Mohammed, money, humanism, capitalism, sex, and the list goes on. Vacuums do not exist in the human mind. Some parents say they will not teach their children about God until they can understand everything. But others are not waiting. Consider Gloria Steinem's challenge, "By the year 2000 we will, I hope, raise our children to believe in human potential, not God."[4]

We live in a society where religious belief is not dictated by the government. Therefore, the spiritual training of our children is left up to us. This provides us with a privilege that others long for even today. For example, in Russia it is illegal to give religious instruction to anyone under eighteen, although freedom of religious worship is guaranteed by the Soviet Constitution. But this same Constitution guarantees freedom of antireligious propoganda. So the Russian is accustomed to blazoned signs in public places like "RELIGION IS THE OPIATE OF THE PEOPLE." Some church buildings and cathedrals have been converted into museums of atheism and *znanie* ("knowledge") societies to combat religion. The *Nauka i Religiya* ("Science and Religion") magazine explains how (supposedly) unscientific religion is.

It is often the Russian grandmothers who take their little grandchildren to worship with them. The Soviet government is not blind to this fact and makes an aggressive effort to educate the grandmothers to atheism. At one such meeting, seventy-eight grandmothers saw children perform experiments "exposing" religion and hear reports on antireligious ideas. Each grandmother was given a leaflet on atheism and a picture of Lenin. At the end of the program the grandmothers promised not to hinder the schools from teaching atheism to the children.[5]

THE BIBLE CAN FILL OUR CHILDREN WITH PEACE, JOY, POWER AND CONFIDENCE IN PRAYER. A constant diet of God's Word can fill their souls until they are overflowing with good things. In the list of the "Christian Graces"

9

in 2 Peter 1:5-7, the first is faith. Faith is the foundation of which all other virtues are built. And how is faith obtained? By hearing God's Word (Romans 10:17). Faith is the beginning of our children's spiritual growth.

ADVANTAGES OF PARENTS TEACHING THEIR OWN CHILDREN

1. Parents have the opportunity to know their children better than anyone else. This is not always true, of course. But who else can see their offspring unfold from a tiny helpless bawling mass of waving arms and legs to a wobbly toddler to a rambunctious preschooler to an enthusiastic school-ager to an awkward adolescent to a mature adult? Who else has the perspective to see his youngster's potential for growth?

Mary, the mother of Jesus, knew her son. Of course, she did not understand everything He did or said but she carefully reflected on His actions. Luke says she "treasured up all these things and pondered them in her heart" (Luke 2:19). From the first announcement of His upcoming birth, she must have thought deeply about how she could bring Christ up in the right way and fulfill her responsibility to God. Jesus was a very special and unique child, the very Son of God. But cannot every parent, "treasure up and ponder" the events, circumstances and needs of their child according to God's Word?

2. Parents can have, in the home, the continuity that no one else can. Unless there are real problems, children come home to the same home and same parents every night. The family eats around the same table every morning and evening. They sleep in the same beds every night. What better place than the home to talk about God's commands when we sit, walk, lie down and get up. Over and over, little by little, the home can mold the habits of a lifetime from childhood to adulthood.

Someone may ask what place these so-called quaint, out-dated Bible stories have in our children's lives with such a rapidly changing, fast-moving society nipping at their heels. So much more do they need the ever-fresh constancy of the Word and they need to receive it in the loving atmosphere of the home.

3. The home has such a great influence over children. This can work for good or evil. Even as young as elementary school, it was difficult for me as a teacher to counteract that influence if a child was in a negative environment at home. Sometimes even diligent work with him would not reap positive results.

When our children are young, they believe everything we say. We have such a responsibility to guide these little ones and to keep training them. Jesus emphasized this when He called a little child to Him: "And whoever welcomes a little child like this in my name welcomes me. But if anyone causes one of these little ones who believes in me to sin, it would be better for him to have a large millstone hung around his neck and to be drowned in the depths of the sea" (Matthew 18:5-6).

4. Children have more security with their parents than anyone else. What other place offers the stability of a mother's lap or a father's hug? Because of this physical closeness, children are more receptive to their parents' words. What better place than the home to unfold God's Word to open hearts!

We can vividly see how this physical and spiritual stability draws families together and entire nations together. There would hardly be a better example of this than the Jewish people, who have survived thousands of years of persecution. The Nazis could burn the Hebrew synagogues but it was difficult for them to end the Sabbath prayer repeated within each Jewish family circle. Imagine the binding effect of this part of the meditation before the kindling of the Sabbath candles:

> *Father of Mercy, O continue thy loving kindness unto me and unto my dear ones. Make me worthy to rear my children that they walk in the way of the righteous before thee, loyal to thy law and clinging to good deeds. Keep thou from us all manner of shame, grief and care; and grant that peace, light, and joy ever abide in our home.[6]*

5. Parents can walk into heaven with their children! After all, that is all that really matters. Designer jeans, sporty cars, expensive houses, honors and achievements will all pass away. But if we can walk into heaven with our children, every effort to teach them the Bible will be worth it.

TOO MUCH?

Is the Lord asking too much of us? Is teaching our children God's Word a reasonable request? After all, we are exhorted to give to the needy, practice hospitality, visit widows and orphans, rejoice, weep, love, and do good to everybody! How will we find the time and the strength?

When Paul pleaded with the Lord that his thorn in the flesh was too much, the Lord replied, "My grace is sufficient for you, for my power is made perfect in weakness" (2 Corinthians 12:9). And so it is with us. With our limited strength we can plant and water God's precious seed in the hearts of our children and know that if we try, God will give the increase. We must remember it is not just our strength. He is "able to do immeasurably more than all we ask or imagine, according to his power that is at work within us" (Ephesians 3:20).

We might feel we have a long row to hoe (or even a heavy hoe to tow!) in our spiritual garden. But God does not ask us to do something we cannot do.

> *He gives strength to the weary and increases the power of the weak. Even youths grow tired and weary, and young men stumble and fall; but those who hope in the Lord will renew their strength. They will soar on wings*

like eagles; they will run and not grow weary, they will walk and not be faint (Isaiah 40:29-31).

Let's get sowing!

CHAPTER 2
BUT I DON'T HAVE A GREEN THUMB!

Digging Deeper

1. What excuses do Christian parents give for not doing a better job of teaching God's Word to their children?

2. Choose a Biblical character and explain in detail how God used him in spite of his excuses and/or his inability. (Examples: Moses, Gideon, Jonah, Ananias, Paul).

3. How important are methods and theories in teaching our children the Bible?

4. What are some ways that save you time and effort so that you can spend more time with the Lord? Share these ideas with others.

5. How can negative motivation, such as guilt, regret, legalism, desperation, and authoritarianism, be detrimental in teaching our offspring God's Word?

6. Search for scriptures that direct parents to teach and train their children.

7. How can the implanted Word, spoken of in James 1:21, save us and then keep saving us?

8. Explain how Christ's ready knowledge of Scripture successfully warded off the temptation from Satan in the wilderness. How can that knowledge do the same for us?

9. How can knowing our children help us teach them better?

10. List the priorities of your life. In what place on your list does teaching the Bible to your children come?

CHAPTER THREE

Planning the Garden

If your plan is for one year, plant rice.
If your plan is for ten years, plant trees.
If your plan is for 100 years, plant education in men.
If your plan is for eternity, plant God in the hearts
  of men.

                    Korean proverb and Becky Tilotta Holbrook

The farmer cannot just plunge in and start tilling up his land to make a garden without some planning. For one thing, he has to figure how large a garden he wants and what crops he hopes to produce. Certain plants take up more room than others. He needs to utilize the areas that would be most advantageous for the crops he plans to grow. He would avoid shady areas since most plants need direct sunlight to grow. If planted alongside each other, tall plants might shade smaller ones. With all these variables, some farmers plot their garden on paper to make sure it will work.

INDISCRIMINATE SPITTING

As the farmer cannot just plunge in, so neither can we as parents dig, throw our Seed to the wind, and hope it brings forth fruit. I am reminded of our next door neighbors when I was a child. Watermelon was their delight. The kids would come to the side porch and spit the seeds into the mound of dirt below. The next summer that spitting of seeds turned into some beautiful watermelons. What a pleasant surprise such "indiscriminate spitting" produced!

Do we expect our children to grow by a likewise "indiscriminate spitting" of the Word? With no plan or purpose—a little Bible class here and there, an occasional youth meeting, a yearly Vacation Bible School, a bit of Bible stories, and a pinch of mealtime prayer—and PRESTO! A Fullgrown Mature Christian emerges? Not so!

It takes a plan to do anything worthwhile and getting to heaven is no exception. In planning to teach our children, we must get our own lives in shape first. Let us compare our lives to the gardener's plan for some insights.

KEEP THINGS STRAIGHT

If the farmer is a disorganized sort of guy, real chaos can break out. If he switches his seed somehow and plants corn where the beans should be or leaves his costly tools in the rain or forgets to harvest his crop, he probably will not remain a farmer long. And it is very important to keep his rows straight so he has some idea where the crops end and weeds begin.

We as Christian parents need to keep things straight. It is not always easy. In spite of all our time-saving devices and more free time, our lives are more hectic and disorganized. Getting organized and "getting it all together" seem to be appropriate for businessman and housewife alike.

We need to get organized spiritually too. Sometimes we wander around in a spiritual forest, knowing our destination is heaven but not having planned our journey to get there. Not that we can know every bump, obstacle or joy in the road either. But at least a plan, using what talents and abilities we discover we have, will make the trip much more purposeful. In this way we can best be utilized in the Lord's work.

Should we be specific in our plans? Yes!

In thinking about our own spiritual lives first, let us do a simple exercise. This is a private perspective of what we think our spiritual life has been so far. On a piece of paper graph your spiritual life. Begin at your baptism and plot the ups and downs as you see them. Has your growth taken a nose dive lately? Was there cause for an upswing in the past? Try to be objective, knowing that this analysis is not set in concrete but just a general idea—a sort of spiritual inventory—of how you see your life. Try to show if growth is steady or sporadic. The examples might give you some idea.

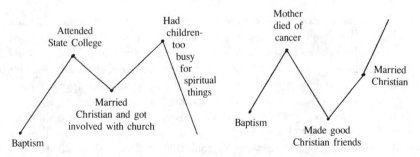

JIM'S SPIRITUAL GRAPH   TRINA'S SPIRITUAL GRAPH

14

Answer these questions to draw some insights from your graphs: Where have I been spiritually? Where am I now? Where am I going? Most importantly, what am I going to do about it?

GOALS AND OBJECTIVES

It would probably help to write down some spiritual goals and objectives for ourselves. Some organizational guides suggest beginning a personal notebook (Anne Ortland's DISCIPLINES OF THE BEAUTIFUL WOMAN is excellent!) Others suggest setting down our lives on 3x5 cards. (SIDETRACKED SISTERS' HAPPINESS FILE by Pam Young and Peggy Jones is super!) You might find an 8x11½ filing system works better for you or a combination of two or three methods. Whichever you choose, make it personal and make it yours.

First, what is your long-range goal? Probably you said HEAVEN. If that is true, then all other goals and objectives should fall parallel to that one principal goal.

Goals are far-reaching and broad. Objectives we could define as "steps to help reach a goal." Gretchen Hirsch in her time management book WOMANHOURS states that an objective, to be complete, must include: "(1.) what you will change, (2). target date for completion, and (3.) a way to determine success. Objectives are always concrete, attainable and measurable."[1]

Here are some examples of spiritual goals and objectives that can work for us in keeping things straight in our spiritual garden.

1. GOAL: To make a daily quiet time with the Lord to read, study, and meditate on His Word and to pray.

OBJECTIVE: In a month from today, to have an appointment with God for at least fifteen minutes a day when the kids settle down for their naps. Successful if I make it five days out of seven. (Behavioralists tell us it takes 21 days of doing something every day to form a habit.)

2. GOAL: To teach a Bible class with confidence.

OBJECTIVE: To teach a class by studying the teacher's manual every week and by helping in another veteran teacher's class. Successful if I can teach the class by myself in three months.

Your goals and objectives might be similar to these or they may not. The point is for you to zero in on your goals and then concentrate on specific ways of attaining them. They do not have to stretch to months or years necessarily. You might feel more comfortable in making weekly goals to start but try eventually to have a long-range target at which to aim.

Make your goals and objectives reasonable. It might be easy to get discouraged because undoubtedly we will fail to meet some of our goals. But it is the continual upward climb that God is interested in—not the occasional slips down the hillside. It is like the backwoods brother who sighed, "I ain't what I should be. I ain't what I could be. But thank God I ain't what I wuz!"

These questions might help you in developing your goals and objectives:
1. How much of the Bible do I know?
2. How many people have I brought to Christ?
3. Is the Christian fruit of the Spirit developing in my life?
4. How am I different from when I first became a Christian?

QUIET TIME WITH GOD

Quiet time with God should be high on our personal priority list of goals. Before we share God's blessings with our children, we have to first fill ourselves with His Word.

CULTIVATING THE RIGHT ATTITUDE—Some approach the Word already knowing what they believe and trying to find one verse to prove them correct. Let us have open hearts and open Bibles! Let our attitudes echo these thoughts: "...Speak, Lord, for your servant is listening..." (1 Samuel 3:9) and "Open my eyes that I may see wonderful things in your law" (Psalms 119:18).

A marvelous example of the right attitude is the righteous man described in Psalm 1:2: "But his delight is in the law of the Lord, and on his law he meditates day and night." Envision this man poring over the scrolls, pondering about what he has read and what it means to him. Do we delight in God's law? Do we meditate upon it?

May the Lord help us develop the hunger and enthusiasm for God's Word, as did the Psalmist: "I open my mouth and pant, longing for your commands" (Psalms 119:131).

MAKING THE TIME—Many Christians feel they cannot take time for study, meditation and prayer. But those who do will confess their day goes much better. Who knows but that a passage read in the morning might help the reader meet a temptation in the afternoon.

Charles Wesley was once asked how he could take out several hours to pray amidst his busy schedule. He replied, "I am so busy, sir, I cannot afford not to take several hours out of my time to pray."[2]

Here are some factors to consider in making the time.

1. MAKE IT REGULAR. Find your best time and keep it. Make your time with God an automatic habit you must do like brushing your teeth or eating a meal. Remember, planning for "sometime" is not enough. Our clocks do not have "sometime" o'clock!

2. MAKE IT EARLY, IF POSSIBLE. Some say, "No Bible, No Breakfast." They do not eat physical food until their spiritual hunger is satisfied. "Very early in the morning, while it was still dark, Jesus got up, left the house and went off to a solitary place, where he prayed" (Mark 1:35). In the morning, we are fresh from a night's sleep and free from ringing phones, screaming children and appointments. If we begin our day with God, He can bless and sustain us the rest of the day.

I met God in the morning
When my day was at its best,
And his presence came like sunrise
Like a glory in my breast.
All day long the presence lingered,
All day long he stayed with me,
And we sailed in perfect calmness
O'er a very troubled sea.
So I think I know a secret
Learned from many a troubled way:
You must seek him in the morning
If you want him through the day!

Ralph Cushman[3]

Others find evening, when the children are in bed, is the only time for them. Some might discover their lunch hour the perfect time to get away from it all. The Lord gave us time. He will help us make that appointment with Him.

3. MAKE IT DAILY. Job said, "I have not departed from the commands of his lips; I have treasured the words of his mouth more than my daily bread" (Job 23:12). Job thought more of God's words than his daily food and so should we. How can we be content to fill ourselves three times a day with physical food and barely make time for Jesus, the Bread of Life? Jesus answered the tempter in the wilderness, "It is written: 'Man does not live on bread alone, but on every word that comes from the mouth of God'" (Matthew 4:4).

"Now the Bereans were of more noble character than the Thessalonians, for they received the message with great eagerness and examined the Scriptures every day to see if what Paul said was true" (Acts 17:11). Their searching did not only consist of busily turning pages three times a week in the worship services. Theirs was a daily exercise due to their "great eagerness." Remember that 15 minutes each day would probably be better than two hours one day a week. The regular feeding on God's Word is healthier for our spiritual bodies just as three meals a day would be better than a daily solitary two hour gorge session! "Blessed are those who hunger and thirst for righteousness, for they will be filled" (Matthew 5:6).

FINDING THE PLACE—Fortunately our devotional lives are not limited to one place. The only limit is a place where we can commune with God and that can be almost anywhere. Sitting at a cleared desk might aid concentration and eliminate distractions. Perhaps you have a roomy closet or comfortable corner in your bedroom. How about the kitchen table? Do you need to get out? Take your Bible to a secluded booth in a restaurant. Go to a lovely meadow. Drive to a panoramic overlook. Walk through a forest.

Wherever your place is, have your family respect it. They should know this is a special time for you and your example will say much as to its importance.

17

Make it easy to read the Bible by carrying it with you when waiting for apppointments or meeting unpunctual people. With Bible stowed under your pillow or closeby, you can read when you awaken early or cannot sleep. Keep the Word in the car for vacations and unexpected traffic jams or repairs. "Remember that the Bible in hand is worth two in the bookcase."[4]

ALLOW FOR INDIVIDUALITY

Another thing the farmer must do to get the most from his garden is to treat each field individually. Fields have different terrains and must be plowed differently. One plot might have a different acid level than another or be more accessible to water. The soil might be gravelly or stony or sandy.

In planning to teach our children God's Word, we must first keep things straight in our own lives by setting priorities. Then the time comes for us to set priorities with our children. Just as each unique soil should be treated differently, we must also allow for our children's differences in setting their goals. Our children, with their various abilities and temperaments, are suited for unique jobs in Christ's kingdom. As parents, our job is to help them find their place in the church and the world.

This is what the writer of Proverbs 22:6 was saying. "Train up a child in the way he should go: and when he is old, he will not depart from it" (KJV). Usually when referring to this verse, we have emphasized the "train up" portion and that definitely is important. But now let us focus on the next part—"in the way he should go." In Hebrew this literally means "in his way." This could be extended to "according to the tenor of his way, i.e. the path specially belonging to, specially fitted for, the individual's character."[5] This does not mean that a child should be left to his own devices to grow like a wild plant. Rather we as parents should train each individual child in the best way he should grow. Just as each member of the church is a unique part of the Body with different functions (1 Corinthians 12:14-27), so each child has a unique destiny to fulfill in God's kingdom. Our question should be "What does God want for my child?" rather than "What do I want for my child?"

Each of our children is different and we should base our expectations accordingly. Can everyone be a preacher? A teacher? A song leader? A Christian writer? A treasurer? A church building custodian? An elder? A deacon? A missionary? Perhaps your child could be all or one or none of these. But it is our job to help our children be exposed to a wide range of interests so they can know in what capacity they can best serve their Lord. Through prayer and a study of the Word, each child can find his niche in the kingdom.

How does this apply to our planning and goal-setting? Does your son show an aptitude in public speaking? Ask the elders about a Timothy class in your congregation. See that your son has opportunities in the Debate Society or Speech

18

Club at school.

Does your daughter show an interest in teaching children? Ask the elders if she might be able to help more experienced teachers in Vacation Bible Schools or other classes.

Does your son show musical talent? Encourage him to lead songs at home, at youth meetings and in his own Bible school classroom. At school the chorus offers opportunities for learning techniques and mechanics of choral singing.

We as parents have to beware lest we impose our choices on our children. We can encourage and leave doors open, but if we start pushing our kids through, trouble will start knocking! A father might live his unfulfilled football career dream through his football playing son, who had rather be fishing! The mother who never had the chance for a "career" might push her daughter into one, although the daughter might be happier as a housewife. A misdirected parent might even try to push his son or daughter into some Christian service for which he or she is not well-suited. More harm would be done to force one to be what he cannot ably be or what he does not want to be. The Lord does not desire that His work be done through the gritting of teeth!

We can begin early with helping our offspring set goals. They can be taught to be helpers around the house as early as the preschool years. Jobs can be posted on a chart, using pictures of the jobs with stickers and/or rewards. (Excellent suggestions for this idea can be found in TRAINING UP A CHILD by Gwendolyn M. Webb, p. 249-259. Other practical but fun approaches can be found in 401 WAYS TO SET YOUR KIDS TO WORK AT HOME by Bonnie Runyan McCullough and Susan Walker Monson.) Or you might choose a job list already prepared. I would like to recommend two: (1) for younger children the "Little Helper Chart," available through mail order from Current, Inc., Colorado Springs, CO 80941 and (2) for school-age children "Young People's Job List," available through Character Builders, 5673 Charleston St., Orlando, FL 32807. Both of these charts include routine tasks like making bed, brushing teeth, hanging up clothes, etc. These charts could be the start of self-discipline and goal-setting in the child.

Now how about some spiritual goal-setting?

For younger children the spiritual goals might be listed on their charts. Here are some examples for a weekly check up:

_____ Read Bible daily

_____ Did a good deed for someone else

_____ Memorized a Bible verse

_____ Invited someone to Bible school

_____ Phoned someone who is sick

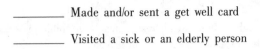

_____ Made and/or sent a get well card

_____ Visited a sick or an elderly person

You might even make the goals
visual by drawing a picture on the
chart. Or make a complete person
each week by coloring in each job as
it is done.[6]

Using the same goal-objective format we noted earlier in the chapter, let us
look at some examples that an older child, perhaps with his parent's help, might
write.

1. GOAL: To memorize a Bible verse a week

OBJECTIVE: In next four weeks to memorize a Bible verse a week by
practicing them ten minutes every day after dinner. Successful if I can say four
verses by heart without mistakes.

2. GOAL: To develop more courage in talking to my friend about Jesus.

OBJECTIVE: By February 1, to have invited five friends to worship services
and have talked to two friends about Christ. Successful if I can do so without
blushing or cowering.

Such goals give children (and parents) something to shoot for. If we have no
goals, how can we measure our progress?

UTILIZE EXPOSURE TO SONLIGHT

Any farmer knows that his plot will not bear crops without sunlight. The intricate
process of photosynthesis depends upon the rays of the sun. The avid indoor
gardener longs for an eastern or southern window so her plants can thrive in the
warm sunlight.

So it is with our Seed and soil. For that Seed to take root in our children soil,
they must feel the daily warmth of the Son—Jesus, God's Son. Jesus affirmed,
"...I am the light of the world. Whoever follows me will never walk in darkness,
but will have the light of life" (John 8:12).

How best can our next generation have this light of life? An obvious answer
is from the exposure to Jesus through the Word which tells of His life, death and

resurrection. But another way is exposure to Jesus through those people, principally parents, who are following the Light. All our teaching and planning for our children is vain if we do not mirror our lives by Jesus' perfect example. As Charles Swindoll stated, "Nothing can really happen through us until it has happened to us."[7] We, as parents, are the reflection of Christ to our children.

The Old Testament is brimming with parents who attempted to provide exemplary role models for their children. Some succeeded, others failed. Let us focus on two of these.

We first meet the elderly priest Eli, sitting by a post in the temple of the Lord in Shiloh. He rebuked Hannah for what seemed to be her drunken rhetoric, when in truth she was praying for a son. Eli told her to "Go in peace" and that the Lord would grant her request. She later bore Samuel and gave him to God for service in the temple. Such sacrificial devotion portrayed by Hannah was not to be found in the family of Eli.

Eli's sons Hophni and Pinehas served as priests and were necessarily taught the Law by their father. But in 1 Samuel 2:12 they are called "wicked men; they had no regard for the Lord." They required the people's sacrifices for themselves before the Lord Himself had a part. They also ". . .slept with the women who served at the entrance to the Tent of Meeting" (1 Samuel 2:22). When Eli heard of his sons' sins, he made a feeble effort at rebuking them. But the time of teaching and training was past. God sent a prophet to warn Eli of his family's coming destruction. Eli was willing to rebuke his sons and he even grieved over their sins. But he was unwilling to give up the wealth that came to him through his sons' misdeeds. The Lord asked Eli, ". . .Why do you honor your sons more than me by fattening yourselves on the choice parts of every offering made by my people Israel?" (1 Samuel 2:29). Eli should have punished his sons by removing them from office. Instead, ". . .he failed to restrain them" (1 Samuel 3:13).

When Hophni and Pinehas looked at Eli, what did they see? Someone just as eager as they were for the riches of their office. Was their exposure to God through Eli a bright and lasting one? No!

On the other hand, Job stood as a shining example to his ten children. His example of patience is well-known to us and must have been one of his outstanding qualities. But let us look at some of Job's other traits that mirrored God to his children.

Job is described in Job 1:1 as "blameless and upright; he feared God and shunned evil." He was not only good to his family but honest and kind in his dealings with others. He not only worshipped God regularly but abstained from evil in his daily life. What a graphic visual object lesson his children saw every day!

But Job's piety did not stop with his own life. His "regular custom" was to sanctify each of his children after their family feasts. Probably these feasts were family get-togethers and not meant for reveling—else why would brothers invite their SISTERS? But just to be sure they had not sinned in their hearts, Job would rise early in the morning and make a sacrifice for each of them. Even as adults, Job's children knew they were sheltered in their father's prayers!

Job's true character was shown when his surviving servants came and told him that all his livestock were gone and his children had been killed. From being the richest man in the East, Job was reduced to poverty. He admitted all belonged to God and confessed, ". . .The LORD gave and the LORD has taken away; may the name of the LORD be praised" (Job 1:21). Job realized that his earthly goods but especially his children were merely loaned to him. They were God's gift for a time for him to mold while in his hands. The great responsibility of this "heritage of the Lord"—his children—caused him to watch his steps ever more closely. Job rose triumphantly over his trials. His children saw their father living right day after day, week after week. What an effect his consistent, positive role of righteousness must have had on his growing children![8]

So we see two fathers—each had the opportunity to mirror the radiance of God to their children. Job accomplished this goal while Eli was a bitter disappointment.

Can our children see the reflection of God in our lives?

CHAPTER 3
PLANNING THE GARDEN
Digging Deeper

1. Write down some spiritual goals and objectives for yourself in a file or notebook. Refer to them daily. How are you carrying out those goals? Revise them if changes are needed.

2. Write down some spiritual goals and objectives for each of your children. If your child is old enough, enlist his help. Perhaps he could record his progress in a tangible way (stickers, stars, etc.)

3. How can writing down goals and objectives help us aim upward and attain our spiritual ideals?

4. Set aside a regular quiet time with the Lord and stuck to it for a week. (Then two weeks, then a month!)

5. In what ways can we cultivate a better attitude when we approach God's Word?

6. Why are shorter periods of daily quiet time spent with the Lord better than longer periods twice a week?

7. Why is it important that your family understand and respect your quiet time?

8. How can our children be taught to consider Christian service as they choose a career, a college, a sport, an activity, a camp, a marriage partner?

9. Give examples of parents in the Bible who succeeded and those who failed to provide exemplary role for their children.

10. Why is it imperative for our children to see Jesus reflected in our lives?

CHAPTER FOUR

Gathering the Tools

"Swing the sickle, for the harvest is ripe..." (Joel 3:13)

In the mind of a gardener, Adam was a lucky guy. Here was this luxuriant garden of all gardens—the Garden of Eden—just begging to be cared for. Even though the garden was "good," it still required someone to prevent overgrowth and disorder. Adam was the one whom the Lord had created to do it (Genesis 2:15).

Have you ever wondered what tools Adam had to work with? Did God create an implement for Adam? Or did Adam design an instrument to till the land or trim the bushes? Of course, we just do not know. But it seems Adam would need some sort of tools.

Gardening tools have come a long way from the ancient implements our ancestors used. We have electric clippers, hedgetrimmers, edgers, lawnmowers, rototillers and tractors for the square-foot garden to the multi-acre spread. The process is basically the same—till the land and plant the seed—but our tools make it a lot easier.

Just as tools make the gardener's work less difficult, so the use of Biblical tools can make teaching our children much easier. Just as the choice of the gardener's tools widens every year so does our selection of Bible tools. Let us look at some of the more useful tools and how we can effectively use them.

But before we run to our nearest Christian bookstore or grab a Christian publishing catalog, let us check out different sources that we might not have considered.

UTILIZE CHURCH LIBRARY

Some brethren provide tools for the yardman and the janitor but the church members are left without adequate aids for Bible study! Fortunately, many congregations are seeing the need and beginning to collect books of interest to their members. The church library, if properly utilized, can be a tremendous help to Bible study.

24

If your congregation does not have a library, talk to the elders about the possibility. Books could be added for a variety of interests and age groups. Bible concordances and dictionaries as well as books on geography, history and languages would be a real boon to the Bible student. A quiet place to study would be an added plus.

What if your church building has no room for a library? One church library began as a "bookcase on wheels," which was rolled out in the vestibule before each service. The teenage girls were assigned before and after service time slots to take care of the library cards. After the members learned the system, they could check out books themselves. The bookcase eventually just stayed in the vestibule.

How can a church with limited funds afford a library? One church held a "library shower." Everyone brought a new or used book. One Christian bookstore even encourages churches to begin their own libraries. They offer a percentage of credit on all materials ordered (Bible school materials, flannelgraph, roll books, etc.) to be put on books for a library. Why not check and see if your bookstore has such an incentive or similar discount?

An alternative to a church library might be a swapping system or perhaps not even a "system" at all. Members who were interested could pass around books that were enjoyable and helpful. Unless a book is extremely valuable or for reference, what good does it do to collect dust on our shelves?

UTILIZE CHURCH RESOURCE ROOM

Known by other names such as "Teachers' Workroom," "Art Room," or "Supply Room," the church resource room is a goldmine for teaching our children. I know. Once another teacher and I cleaned one out. Only other packrats like myself could appreciate the delight I experienced! Unfortunately, there were some things so old or outdated that even packrats could not use. Sadly some of the Lord's money goes for postcards we never send, Bible school material we never use, and costly visual aids we use once and then never use again for lack of proper care or adequate storage. Are we not stewards in this area too? Will we not be held accountable?

It is time for parents to discover this source of materials that teachers have put to use for years. The parent is HELPING the Bible school teacher by teaching his child, not tramping on the "teacher's territory." The use of puppets, filmstrips, and flannelgraph in the home might take some of the novelty away from the classroom situation but who tells the same story in an identical way? Perhaps there could be an agreement for payment for damaged/lost materials before they are checked out. It is far better to wear materials out by teaching than to let them "rust out" or become outdated.

UTILIZE PUBLIC LIBRARY

When I worked in a public library, I was pleasantly surprised at the selection of religious books, especially for children. There must have been regular contributions of religious books by interested individuals. A library might not buy a religious book but it might be more difficult to turn down a gift which is up-to-date and appealing. (This is one way you might have to make an impact on spirituality in the public library—contribute a good book. In this way, many more people might have access to this book than you might be able to reach personally.)

For the cost of a library card, you can broaden your range of religious reading or see if a book is worthy enough to buy. Sometimes you can find out what denominations are teaching by checking out their books without investing in their materials. Many libraries have Bible dictionaries and atlases that might be of use. It is imperative, however, to use care when the opinion of men is considered, as in commentaries.

We must be extremely careful of feeding our minds on false teaching. There is a time and place for investigating the beliefs of others, but it is certanly not when one is not firm in his own faith. As parents we can control to an extent what our children read. We should exercise that prerogative. Babes are not ready for meat and young people are not always ready for controversial and erroneous books. Then again, some books are not worth reading by anyone—period!

Some public libraries carry tapes and records on Biblical stories which might be beneficial in teaching our children. Others maintain active vertical files on different religious beliefs.

I found the variety and creativity in the children's section helpful in teaching my own children. There are Bible story books that cover the entire Bible or main events while others concentrate on one character or one period of history. Some highlight the text; others emphasize illustrations. There are books about topics like prayer and faith. Any of these selections could supplement your Bible teaching at home.

When examining these books, it is helpful to be aware of the religious affiliation of the publisher. It is good to know where the author is coming from and the publisher can give you a big clue. Several large religious publishers are Baker, Zondervan, Revell, and Eerdmans. Standard Publishing Company, which has excellent illustrated books as well as visual aids, is affiliated with the Christian Church. Warner Press is connected with the Anderson, Indiana, branch of the Church of God. The Review and Herald Publishing Association is the publishing arm of the Seventh Day Adventist Church. They publish beautifully illustrated Bible story books, found in almost every dentist's and doctor's office.

Any religious book written by man should be closely screened by parents. The public library offers the opportunity to do just that. Check it out!

UTILIZE RELIGIOUS BOOKSTORE

Gone are the days when all the religious bookstore carried were Bible school curriculum, Bibles and hymnbooks. Besides that, they now have toys, pictures and plaques with Christian themes, bible picture coloring and sticker books, Bible games, greeting cards, religious videos, and books on family life, child rearing and other topics of interest. And that is just a start!

You are especially blessed if you have a local Christian bookstore operated by members of the church. Please support it! Make regular visits to see what is new. Keep up with the latest visual aids. Think of it when gift-giving occasions arrive—do not forget anniversaries, Mother's Day, and Father's Day. See if they have any discount plan whereby they could help you start a church library. If you want something they do not have, perhaps they can order it.

If you are not fortunate enough to live close to a Christian bookstore, plan a trip to one and make it fun. Visit before the kids are worn out from the day's activities. Allow each child to pick out one thing he would like. While they are deciding, you will have time to look over some gift ideas for them later (and maybe for yourself too!)

If visiting a Christian bookstore is not possible, write for a catalog. Some bookstores do not send out catalogs but a major Christian publisher will be happy to send one. The advantage is that you see everything the publisher carries with price and description. The disadvantage is that you cannot peruse the books, feel the puppets nor hear the recordings. That is why it is helpful to take the time to visit if at all possible.

UTILIZE OTHER SOURCES

Do not forget unlikely sources for teaching material. I have found nice Bible puzzles and books at garage sales and discount stores. My husband and I are hopeless bibliophiles and love to haunt old book sales. You never know what you will find until you look!

UTILIZE PERSONAL LIBRARY

There are two principal mistakes Christians make in gathering their Biblical tools. Some Christians use their Bible exclusively without taking advantage of the many helps that are available. Others depend on their tools so much that they do not have much time to study the Word itself! Let us find a balance.

What are some worthy additions to your personal library?

BIBLE

A sword—that is what Paul called the Word of God (Ephesians 6:17). "The sword of the spirit" is our most important tool because it is our guide to heaven. All other aids are based on it. No wonder the writer of Hebrews penned, "For the word of God is living and active. Sharper than any double-edged sword, it penetrates even to dividing soul and spirit, joints and marrow; it judges the thoughts and attitudes of the heart" (Hebrews 4:12).

A mother was trying to review this "sword" idea of God's Word with her young son. When he looked blank, she gave him a clue. "It's something that cuts, something that's very sharp." He lit up and said, "Of course—the axe of the apostles!"

Be sure you find an accurate and readable translation with which you can feel at home. Find a Bible you can write in and take with you wherever you go. If you have sight problems, find one with big print, on tape or in Braille. Do not let anything stop you from filling your mind with God's message. Make the Bible yours and do not "abuse" it.

BIBLE ABUSE?

Two Bibles were brought to church one day
And placed down on the pew.
One was worn from constant use;
The other good as new.

A member said, "That poor Bible!
It's neglected so and worn.
The other is so clean and new.
It puts the other to scorn!"

"Oh, no!" another member said.
"The new one is abused.
Sitting on the shelf all week,
It's hardly ever used.

The Bible worn and ragged
From daily study and wear
Will lead its owner to heaven one day
To riches bright and fair."

So take care of YOUR Bible.
Make sure it isn't abused.
Don't lay it aside to gather dust.
Make sure that it is used!

Nancy Eichman

Some people find Bibles with cross-references, dictionaries, maps and concordances helpful with their study. It depends on what other aids you intend to buy. Keep in mind that usually the more helps a Bible contains, the slightly heavier it gets. Do not buy one that is so heavy that you are unwilling to carry it to church or anywhere else. Usually dictionaries and concordances in the backs of Bibles are limited because of space. Just the same, I find my cross-references, concordance and maps indispensable for study away from home when I cannot check the bigger, separate volumes. Some people prefer study Bibles, with concise notes explaining scripture, or parallel Bibles, with comparative versions on facing pages. Ask your minister or elders what they suggest.

OTHER TOOLS

In buying our other tools it is good not to rush and all at once buy everything that appeals to us. Just as a wise gardener builds his tool collection slowly according to his needs, so should the Christian carefully build his religious library. Use church and public libraries to know which authors you find most helpful. It is better to find out beforehand than to buy books that you hardly use. Consider your needs and find whatever suits your purposes.

Here are some suggestions for building your own library.

1. CONCORDANCE. When you do not know where a verse is found but you know a key word or phrase, a concordance is a must. It can also be used as a springboard for word studies.

2. COMMENTARIES. Lack of money or space may prevent you from buying a complete set of commentaries. (This is where the church library set of commentaries comes in!) Check on the one-volume commentaries for each Old and New Testament. If you do choose to buy a complete set, be sure the author or editor is basically conservative in his thinking. Commentaries are not much help if you have to spend precious time weeding out false doctrine. As one brother aptly put it, "The Bible sure sheds a lot of light on those commentaries!" Your minister, elders or Bible school teacher can probably tell you their preferences. You also might choose to do what my husband does—pick up separate volumes at book sales and closeouts. You might not want to get a commentary on every book—perhaps just the New Testament, Genesis, Minor Prophets and others.

3. DICTIONARY. A Bible dictionary is vital to understanding the obsolete words and customs of Bible times. Some dictionaries, written especially for children, include maps, photos and illustrations.

4. ENCYCLOPEDIAS. These usually come in sets but not always. The article entries are longer and more extensive than dictionary entries. These would be helpful for a thorough knowledge of a topic. You probably would not need both a dictionary and encyclopedia but whichever would suit your needs best.

5. ATLAS. Many Bibles contain the general maps helpful for clarifying Bible places. If you choose a separate atlas, make sure the maps are well-defined and colorful so you can use them with your children too. Going "up to Jericho" makes much more sense when you can see the topography of Palestine!

6. BIBLE HANDBOOK/ALMANAC. These general comprehensive guides might be helpful for outlines of the books of the Bible, history, culture and countless

other information.

7. GOSPEL HARMONY. Have you ever tried to find the same miracle of Jesus or another account of the crucifixion in another gospel? This is the purpose of the gospel harmony—to "harmonize" the four gospels side by side for comparison.

8. GENERAL REFERENCE. There are Surveys, Introductions, a sort of Biblical who's who (from Aaron to Zurishaddai!) and even BOOKS ABOUT THE BOOK: A GUIDE TO BIBLICAL REFERENCE WORKS! As your Bible study increases, these might be valuable additions to your Biblical library.

9. BIBLE STORY BOOK. About the time some child starts chiming "Read me a story!" their parents think to put "Bible Story Book" on their shopping list (under "training pants" and "toys"!) Unfortunately sometimes more care is taken with choosing the brand of training pants and the variety of toy than is taken with selecting a quality Bible story book! Since Bible story books come in literally all shapes and sizes, a parent can easily become overwhelmed with the variety. Let us concentrate on those that span the entire history of the Bible. Perhaps some guidelines can help us be more discriminating.

"Guidelines for Selecting a Bible Story Book"

1.) Is it scriptural? This is of foremost importance because you do not want to have to "unexplain" everything to your kids. Check certain stories and/or pictures where error might be taught. Sometimes in pictures portraying Pentecost or the baptism of Jesus, baptism is shown as sprinkling or pouring. A lamb and a lion are pictured standing with a child in one popular story book, clearly portraying the author's belief in the erroneous earthly, literal fulfillment of Isaiah's prophecy.

2.) Will it appeal to the age and personality of my child? I believe the best books can be enjoyed several years for a variety of purposes. Certain books have definite age limits while others appeal to specific personalities.

3.) Are the illustrations frequent, interesting and colorful? I personally prefer a picture on every other page so that the child can look at something while I am reading. Younger children prefer simpler illustrations.

4.) Is the Bible portrayed as fact or fable, miracle or myth? Sometimes the author's erroneous viewpoint may be masked by lovely illustrations. You cannot judge a Bible story book by its cover—or its illustrations!

10. CHRISTIAN PERIODICALS. You can tell much about a person by what he reads. "For as he thinketh in his heart, so is he. . ." (Proverbs 23:7 KJV). Christian periodicals such as bulletins, magazines and tabloids fill our minds with the "right stuff"—whatever is true, noble, right, pure lovely, admirable, excellent and praiseworthy (Philippians 4:8). A simple absence of pornographic materials is not enough. We must fill that void with quality reading. Our children will perceive that spiritual things are more important to us by the magazines we read.

The frequency of these publictions serves another purpose. By receiving these several times a year, we can keep up-to-date on information about the brotherhood. Besides the articles written by Christians on Bible subjects, there are reports of workshops, gospel meetings, campaigns, debates, youth meetings, and lectureships. By becoming aware, we will be more prepared to help if our asistance is needed, financially or otherwise. Our children will see that the church does not only exist in their home congregation. We have a world mission and periodicals can keep that before us.

UTILIZE A FILING SYSTEM
FOR RELIGIOUS MATERIALS

Remember how we saw the need to "keep things straight" in planning our garden? This is probably never needed more than in keeping up with the mass of religious material that can bombard us from all sides. What do we do with the church bulletins, children's Bible school take-home papers and all those little attendance cards from the back of the pew that we scribble notes from Sunday morning's lesson? An easy solution is to throw everything in the round file and be done with it. But wait!

It is possible that you will never use some of those items that were mentioned so why save them—for yourself, that is. But could someone else gain from the bulletins we pitch in the wastebasket? Local church bulletins are mostly of interest to the local members. How about occasionally sending one to a former member who has moved away? A friend did that for us and we enjoyed keeping up with the congretion. Is there a poem or article you like that might help someone else? Cut it out and send it to them. Is there an explanation you would like to refer to again? Cut it out and file it.

You do not have to have a fancy system with an expensive file cabinet. You can use cardboard file boxes or make them out of laundry detergent boxes, covered with contact paper. As for titling your entries, just use geneal headings at first; then you can get more specific later. You might start with "BAPTISM." Then when that file gets too full, break it down with BAPTISM—INFANT or BAPTISM—IMMERSION.

Seems a little tedious, this filing system? Think—if we do not have a system for keeping it, what happens to that article or poem if we ever want it again? Gone—many times forever. If you know you can retrieve it later in some book or other source, fine. But if you cannot, it is lost for good. Solomon's statement in Ecclesiastes 3:6 is appropriate here! "A time to search, and a time to give up as lost; A time to keep, and a time to throw away."

Filing takes the worry out of keeping up with things. Better filed than getting all ratty and torn, sticking out of our Bibles. Better filed than "somewhere in the papers on my desk." Better filed than laying around for Junior to eat or draw on!

31

How about the sermon notes written on the attendance cards? Next time bring a notebook so you can write your notes large enough to read! Meanwhile transfer what you can on larger paper to file away.

Really now—should we save childen's take homes? Yes—and no. Yes, if the picture is so colorful that you can use it again in teaching your children or Bible class. Yes, if the art or craft idea is so unique you will use it again. These could be filed according to story or general area of Bible history such as Genesis, Israelite judges, or kings. Or they could be hole-punched in a notebook with dividers. If you must throw them away, first display them on the refrigerator or memo board so you can review the lesson with your child and praise him on his work.

A filing system need not become a catch-all for what you do not know what to do with, either. We borrow a term from gardening—"weeding"—to discard the excess that we do not want or need. Weed every six months to a year—and hopefully your file cabinet will not burst assunder!

UTILIZE YOUR OWN "IMAGINALITY"

What is "imaginality"? (I have borrowed this term from Patrick and Beverly Scott and Jana Smith, who have produced a creative series of books of ingenious ideas for classroom games and visual aids. These books can be adapted to teaching your kids at home.) Imaginality is a combination of imagination and originality and it suits our purpose here well. Our creativity is a valuable tool for teaching our children.

Someone might say, "Are you kidding? I don't have any imagi-whatever!" Wait! God has blessed every person with some imaginality—it is just more developed in some people than others. We all start out as creative little dynamos with unique views of the world. Just look at a baby or young toddler! Years of conforming to the norm leaves much of that creativity stifled behind in our childhood.

When those imaginality wheels start turning in our heads, they might be a little rusty at first. Not every idea will be brilliant nor will each idea always work. But our children will appreciate our efforts and God will bless us. It reminds me of the mother who hit upon an idea to get across the difficult concept of the Godhead. She excitedly ran to the kitchen and brought out an egg. "Imagine that God is the yolk. Jesus is the white. And the Holy Spirit is the shell. They all combine to make one." To demonstrate what she meant, she broke the shell into a bowl and out came a double-yolk egg![1]

With our tools in hand, let's start digging!

CHAPTER 4
GATHERING THE TOOLS
Digging Deeper

1. What materials do other parents use in their personal Bible study and in the teaching of their children?

2. What are the possibilities of a church library in your congregation? If you presently have one, how could it be up-dated and expanded to reach the needs of more members?

3. Is a parent teaching God's Word to his child at home tramping on the Bible school "teacher's territory"?

4. What religious books and tapes are available in your public library?

5. Why is it necessary for us to be aware of the books our children are reading?

6. Where is your nearest religious bookstore? If the bookstore is too far for a visit, are you receiving a bookstore or publisher's catalog?

7. Explain what the writer of Hebrews 4:12 meant when he compared the Word to a sword in its penetrating and judging capacities.

8. What Christian periodicals do you subscribe to at home? What is the number of Christian periodicals received compared to the total number of periodicals you receive? How many does the church provide for its members?

9. Why do you think we often feel that we are not very creative?

10. With the recommendations of others and your own observations, what are the best tools you could use in your family? Write them down for later reference.

Bible _____

Concordance _____

Commentaries _____

Dictionary _____

Encyclopedia _____

Atlas _____

Handbook/Almanac _____

Gospel Harmony _____

General Reference_____

Bible Story Book _____

Christian Periodicals_____

CHAPTER FIVE

A Little Help
From Our Friends

"For we are God's fellow workers..." (I Corinthians 3:9)

What gardener, however proficient he might be, has not learned a helpful tidbit or two from a neighbor or friend? When we lived in Portland, Oregon, we were eager for a luscious tomato crop like we had enjoyed in Indiana. However, our garden was blessed in Portland with something we did not have in Indiana—SLUGS! The icky slimy creatures had a notorious reputation for cutting the plants at the root. What should one do to combat these offensive night marauders?

Our friends to the rescue! Each had a way he coped with the hideous creatures. One suggested putting salt around the edge of our garden plot. Another recommended the use of his favorite brand of pesticide called "SLIME THE SLUG" (or something like that!) Another friend said the best way to be sure they were gone was to do it yourself. So every night about "slug coming out time," he would take his trusty flashlight and head for his garden in anticipation of his favorite outdoor sport "TUG-A-SLUG," consisting of picking off the slugs and smushing them!

A little help from our friends can come in handy, whether we are raising tomatoes or children. Though teaching our children God's Word is primarily our responsibility, we need all the help we can get! Let us look at some of the friends we can call on for help in this important task.

HELP FROM OUR EXTENDED FAMILY

Gone are the days when most children had their grandparents, aunts, uncles, and cousins living in the same house or nearby. In fact, many of today's families see their relatives only a few times a year. Time and distance have made it hard for a relative to form a close attachment and become a "significant other." What spiritual help could be gained from someone so far away?

A relative might live in a distant city but that does not have to negate his godly influence. I remember an aunt and uncle who will always mean a great deal to me spiritually. Because of distance, I saw them quite infrequently but their Christian sweetness and goodness will remain with me always. From the time I was a young child, they took the time to listen and encourage me to do good. I will not forget their influence on my life.

With our transient society, it will take more effort for families to stay in touch spiritually. When we contact each other by phone or letter, why not mention a verse or spiritual thought or encouragement? Why not give "spiritual gifts," i.e. presents that can encourage one another in a spiritual way? Going to buy a coloring book? Occasionally make it about Jesus, our "Master of the Universe." How about a puzzle? Make it a Bible one. Your niece into romances? Pick up some of the religiously oriented romances directed at young people. Find plaques and books with spiritual emphasis for other relatives. Ask them to pray for a special need. (You can do that over the phone.) Ask them to praise God for a special answer to prayer. We can share spiritually—even if it is by long distance!

When relatives do visit, it is an opportune time for letting them share their walk with God, beginning with their childhood. What or who encouraged them to be good when they were little? When and where did they become Christians? How has God led them through trials, tragedies and triumphs? All this could be recorded on tape or put down in a book entitled "God in Our Family" or "Our Spiritual Heritage."

Conversely, some relatives live close enough to share their spirituality more frequently. What an influence for good they can have! Somehow devotions and family rituals take on greater meaning when they are shared with more than the nuclear family. As a grandchild looks up and sees her aged grandparents worshipping the same God she does, it gives her a sense of her spiritual heritage. The Jewish people, resiliant after centuries of persecution, are bound together by their rich spiritual heritage, passed down generation to generation.

Just like Eunice encouraged her daughter Lois and her grandson Timothy, grandparents have the opportunity to encourage two generations. Grandparents can serve as examples to the young as to how they can serve God in their later years. The gray-haired one might have slower steps but he can still grow spiritually. My dear grandma never lost her joy in worshipping God. My faithful grandpa led singing until health forced him to sing in the pew. What a special place these people hold in our hearts and how they influence us!

Sadly, every member in our outer family (or inner family, for that matter) may not be faithful Christians. It is difficult to teach children about godly things when their grandparents smoke, drink and swear before them. Then there are children who have lost their love for God while the Christian grandparents gaze at their spiritually neglected grandchldren.

One of our greatest blessings would be to have strong Christian ties with our extended family. But it does not always happen, even with diligent concern and prayer. Let us do what we can to reach our relatives. We can pray for them. We can teach them the truth in love. We can show by our example that God means everything to us. And whatever happens, we can trust that God will reward us for our efforts—they are not in vain.

Relatives can help parents plant the Seed and the roots can go deep and strong to last for generations. It takes effort on our part. We can trust our God to give the increase.

HELP FROM OTHER CHRISTIANS

There is much that other Christians can do to help us teach our children God's Word. Here are some ideas to consider.

The preacher can do much to emphasize the Bible study habit. He can give the congregation time to find the scriptures pertinent to his sermon. Varying his sermons between textual and topical studies and between the Old and New Testament will give the congregation a well-rounded diet of the Scriptures. He can preach sermons on Bible reading and encourage families to hold Bible devotions in their homes. A congregational Bible reading plan would offer an opportunity for the preacher to preach a textual study from the past week's study. The preacher or another interested Christian could spend ten to thirty minutes before each Sunday night service with the preschool and school-age children in Bible drills, games, songs and films.

What about memorizing scriptures together as a congregation? The Bible school teacher could use various methods to introduce them in class and parents could follow up at home. With everyone learning together, the job would be easier. Then on Sunday the congregation could say the verse in unison.

Timothy classes and Men's Leadership classes can give men and boys more confidence and experience in leading the public worship. This training can lead to more thoughtful worship for the whole congregation. If there is not enough interest for a long-term class, why not make a concentrated effort for a month of Sundays or weeknight series.

Dorcas classes for girls can combine the practical aspects of sewing, cooking and cleaning for others with the spiritual study of the Word. Ladies Bible classes can serve the same purpose.

How about special concentrated Bible teaching sessions primarily aimed at a textual study of the Word, like "Through the Bible in Three Days"? Some lectureships concentrate on single books of the Bible with different speakers. How about men in the congregation taking a book of the Bible and giving its highlights?

The church could provide a home study packet, full of quizzes, puzzles and other goodies, for parents to work with their children at home. Different families could gather the ideas to use and the church could copy them for all the members. Or how about a BIBLE GAZETTE, which includes Bible games and articles for home devotionals. This could be written by members or the young people on a rotating basis.

The church or individual classes could give New Testaments or Bibles to graduating classes of kindergarten, sixth grade and twelfth grade. The Bibles could be chosen according to age level, i.e. a large print New Testament with illustrations for the beginning reader. This gift, personalized with the recepient's name, could be incorporated into a ceremony commemorating "landmarks" in spiritual growth. Hopefully, this would encourage him to make his Bible study personal.

HELP FROM BIBLE SCHOOL TEACHERS

We should never underestimate the influence that Bible teachers can have in our children's spiritual lives by their teaching and example. Just note the biblical examples of those who filled this need. Eli played such a role for Samuel, who in turn, influenced the young man David. Elisha looked to the older Elijah for guidance. The priest Jehoiada, while he lived, influenced the seven year old Joash to do right at a wicked time in Judah's history.

We can probably think of a special Bible teacher (or two or three) who has helped us in the past on our spiritual journey. Jane McWhorter tells of two influential Bible teachers in her life. One helped lay foundations for further learning by stressing facts. This teacher was a great help in her further Bible study. In contrast, the other teacher had no visual aids and stressed no lists or facts. Jane writes:

. . .To this woman, however, God was very real. He was her daily companion. Through the tone and sincerity of her voice, I also became acquainted with her Bible friends. They were so real that I could almost feel the burning sand under my own feet as the Israelites wandered in the wilderness. When she compassionately told of Aaron and Hur as they supported the arms of Moses in the battle with the Amalekites, my own arms ached with the weariness which Moses must have felt. I even wonder how manna must have tasted. In my imagination, I took each step with God's people during those 40 years. It is to this Bible teacher that I give the credit for instilling within me a deep love for studying the Scriptures.[1]

We cannot deny that the preparation of lessons and the stressing of facts and lists are important in teaching our children. But we pray that teachers will go beyond that to demonstrate a genuine love for God and His Word that their students can see and emulate. What role models these teachers could be! We hope our children will be blessed with a teacher displaying these qualities.

A TEACHER'S "BE ATTITUDES"

Blessed (happy) are the teachers who teach my child for they make our road to heaven easier and my teaching load a little lighter.

Blessed (happy) is he who is faithful in his attendance so that my child develops trust in the same person week after week.

Blessed (happy) is she who loves God and His Word so much that her enthusiasm for them overflows to the heart of my child.

Blessed (happy) is he who takes a personal interest in every child so that each one feels important.

Blessed (happy) is she who prepares her lesson for the age level of her students so they will understand God's great truth.

Blessed (happy) is he who does not force my child to pray or lead singing or read Scripture but rather encourages him to take part.

Blessed (happy) is she who saves extra material and take-homes for visitors and new class members so they can feel more welcome.

Blessed (happy) is he who offers incentives (Bible related games, stickers, puzzles, etc.) for memorizing scriptures and bringing visitors for he is encouraging good habits.

Blessed (happy) is she who truly expects her students to learn and gives them quizes to test their knowledge and her teaching.

Blessed (happy) is he who encourages his students to participate in Bible Bowls and Testament Tournaments for these activities, held in the right spirit, can build their Bible knowledge.

Blessed (happy) is she who lets her students answer the roll in learning ways such as saying a Bible verse or answering a Bible question for she is using her brief teaching time wisely.

Blessed (happy) is he who encourages his students to do their Bible homework so the parent may reinforce learning at home.

Blessed (happy) is she who is genuinely friendly to me as a parent because my child will more easily learn to trust her.

Blessed (happy is he who is receptive to new ways of teaching and learning.

Blessed (happy) is she who maintains an attractive classroom, primarily for the reason of teaching God's Word better.

Blessed (happy) is he who encourages deeper study in the classroom by providing copies of Bibles, concordances, song books, and maps for reference.

Blessed (happy) are they who teach and train my children in the Bible classroom; may God richly bless them and their efforts.

PLANNING AHEAD FOR WORSHIP

For many Christian families, Sunday is not a happy day of worship but a hectic day of tenson and frustration. The attitude of your family when they arrive at services has much to do with how much they will get out of worship. If they are huffing and puffing from the harum-scarum Sunday Morning Scramble, it will take them half of class time to catch their breath. On the other hand, a calm, collected family is more receptive to worship and to learn from the Word.

I can speak from personal experience. One New Year's Eve at an early family devotional, each of our family was telling one good quality of every other family member and a personal quality of our own that we felt needed improvement. I admitted, "Well, I think I need to try harder to be ready to leave for church." My six year old son, trying to be encouraging but speaking more frankly than he knew, said, "Mom, I remember when you were on time—once!"

It was not that I made our family walk in after Bible classes had begun. It was just that my timing was causing my family anxiety and needless waiting, while I finished doing things I felt were necessary.

But all rationalizations aside, we worked on a plan to help us all get ready on time. We found we could do a lot on Saturday evening to make Sunday less rushed. Then even if we had to take a detour on the way or the baby spits up on Aunt Martha's heirloom pinafore (it never fails!), we will not be so timed to the second that we still can arrive at church in one piece. Maybe this could help you.

Saturday Evening Checklist

1. Put out Sunday clothes.
2. Put out contribution. (Kids too.)
3. Do Bible lesson.
4. Put Bibles, lessons, Worship Bag, contribution in one place, preferably near exit.
5. Take baths.
6. Be sure everyone is in bed at a decent hour.
(Some parents plan their Family Nights for Saturday nights so they can govern their children's bedtime.)

Sunday Morning Checklist

1. Easy-to-fix breakfast
2. No TV (or until ready)
3. No Sunday comics (or until ready)

We prepare for things that are important. That is why God set aside a "get ready day" for the all important Sabbath. This Day of Preparation was lived looking to tomorrow. God's idea of preparing ahead was a good one. Let us use it!

DURING WORSHIP

By encouraging our child to participate as much as he can, we can prevent behaviour problems and help him get more out of worship. He can sing the songs, even if he does not know every word. For the younger child learning to read, it might be helpful to follow the words in the songbook with your finger. We take so much for granted in following the notes and markings because we have sung the songs for years. It might be a little confusing for a child! We can also help him find the Scriptures the minister uses in his sermon.

WORSHIP AFTERMATH

We might be sure to get our children to Bible classes on time. But what happens when we step out the church house doors? Could we hear the following conversation in the car on the way home?

"Oh Henry, the sermon was so boring! That must be the twelfth lesson on 'giving' this year. Doesn't the preacher know we're about given out?"

"Well, Henrietta, I just about fell asleep because the building was so hot. Don't the deacons know how to control that thermostat?"

"Asleep? How could you sleep? That tacky-looking visitor from across the tracks kept coughing so loudly I could hardly hear anything. Can't the elders do something about these ill-behaved people, interrupting our worship like that?"

"Come to think of it, I did hear something. It was so funny that I could hardly keep a straight face. Did you hear that brother 'what's his name' read scripture? He was a riot! He lisped and stuttered and turned so red!"

"And the songleader always pitches the songs too high or too low. The rest of the time he's off-key. The congregation can't seem to follow too well either."

"Well, I just hope next Sunday will be better. But then—what will we have to talk about after services? Oh—children," as he turned to the backseat, where little eyes and ears had not missed a word of the conversation, "what did YOU get out of church today?"

Henry and Henrietta might be headed for a restaurant for their Sunday lunch but they have already sufficiently roasted the preacher, fried the songleader, baked the deacons, fricasseed the elders and shish-ka-bobbed everyone else. What a menu for a healthy outlook on the church! What better diet to burn up any enthusiasm for working with God's people!

A friend once said she never heard her father speak ill of anyone. Parents like that are difficult to find. We might not find it easy to "hold our tongues" before our children, but now is the time to start. Church members are not perfect but our children will see their faults enough without our weekly derogatory character analysis.

What is an alternative to this Sunday "after-church barbeque"? How about asking each other questions like: "What was the main idea of the sermon? What was your Bible class about? Do you have a new memory verse to learn? Who was absent from the assembly today? Could we call them to see if they might need something?" Any negative comments could be dealt with but not emphasized.

We can reinforce our child's Bible school activities by asking him to tell us about it. Listen for feedback so you will know were to fill in the "blanks" or clear up misunderstandings. Especially is this important for the younger child. One child was confused by the story of Lot. His teacher told the class that Lot was warned to take his wife and daughters and flee out of Sodom before it was destroyed. The little boy asked his parents later, "What happened to the flea?" Or consider the little girl who proudly showed her Mom and Dad her drawing of a multicolored goat—Joseph's GOAT of many colors! Or there is the little one who had it all figured out—the apostles married epistles and had baby oppossums!

If possible, save your young child's take-homes for a month at a time and put them in a special place, perhaps a notebook. Review his lessons periodically. Check with his teacher to learn what songs he sings in class (it would be great if she provided a list) and practice those at home. Complement your child's activities at church by your interest at home.

DOING OUR PART TO HELP EACH OTHER

How else can we do our part?

1. We can cooperate in the many activities of the church and encourage our child to take part.

2. We can encourage others in the church to become caring influences on our child.

3. We can get to know church leaders better so our children can see them "up close and personal."

4. We can share our devo ideas and experiences with other Christians.

5. We can teach in the church program ourselves for a three way benefit—our students, our children and us!

6. We can pray within our family circle for the church leaders, teachers, preachers, and members.

Extended family and friends can greatly encourage our children in their study of God's Word and their quest for spiritual maturity. We as parents can encourage or negate that influence. Let us willingly utilize all the help we can get!

HELP FROM OUR BEST FRIEND

In the great gardening chapter of the Bible, Christ begins, "I am the true vine and my Father is the gardener" (John 15:1). Again in verse 5, He says, "I am the vine; you are the branches. If a man remains in me and I in him, he will bear much fruit; apart from me you can do nothing." In these verses we see the total reliance we have on our very Best Friend—Jesus—to bear fruit. And bearing fruit is what gardening is all about.

But later in the chapter Christ highlights the three-way friendship that should exist to make our spiritual gardens truly fruitful. That triangle involves Christ,

41

others and us as individuals. With all of us working together, a more bountiful harvest is insured! Speaking to His disciples, our Lord said,

My command is this: Love each other as I have loved you. Greater love has no one than this, that one lay down his life for his friends. You are my friends if you do what I command. I no longer call you servants, because a servant does not know his master's business. Instead, I have called you friends, for everything that I learned from my Father I have made known to you. You did not choose me, but I chose you to go and bear fruit—fruit that will last. Then the Father will give you whatever you ask in my name. This is my command: Love each other (John 15:12-17).

CHAPTER 5
A LITTLE HELP FROM OUR FRIENDS
Digging Deeper

1. What relatives encouraged you or someone in your immediate family to live godly and how?

2. What are some ways that you could make a spiritual impact on "long distance" relatives?

3. Why is it important for the congregation to receive a well-rounded diet of the scriptures from their preachers and teachers?

4. Name Bible characters who greatly influenced their younger followers for good or evil.

5. What Bible teachers have meant a great deal to you and why?

6. What do you feel are the qualities of an outstanding Bible school teacher?

7. Name some ways you can better prepare for worship on Sundays and Wednesdays.

8. Find out what the Day of Preparation, the day before Sabbath, involved.

9. How can we positively reinforce learning after worship services?

10. How can we help our children from feeling "down" on the church when they see the faults of church members?

CHAPTER SIX

The Ever Viable Seed

Who plants a seed beneath the sod
And waits to see believes in God.

Author Unknown

The length of time a seed is viable or capable of germinating varies from plant to plant. Some seeds require careful harvesting and storing to retain their viability while others remain viable for years with no special care. Years ago a Japanese botanist discovered lotus seeds in a dry Manchurian lake. Some experts claim they had been there 300-400 years. Others insist they were over a thousand years old. The amazing thing is that when these lotus seeds were planted, most of them germinated!

Some seeds are viable a short time; others might be viable a thousand years. But we can hold spiritual SEED in our hands that is ever viable, ever living—everlasting and eternal. That Seed is the Word of God. The book that some men think of as an out-of-date collection of fables, history, and poetry, is still changing lives and saving men. This "Energized Word" has the power to do that whenever or wherever it is found. When planted in a good heart, the Seed can produce a plentiful harvest.

Historically, conditions have not always been the best for God's Word to survive. Men have burned the Bible and those who possessed it but they could not burn up God's message. Rulers forbade its use and the printing of its copies but they could not yank its message from the hearts of believers. God's precious Seed has survived countless attacks until now and it will remain.

Peter, referring to the Seed, wrote:

"For you have been born again, not of perishable seed, but of imperishable, through the living and enduring word of God. For, 'All men are like grass, And all their glory is like the flowers of the field; the grass withers and the flowers fall, but the word of the Lord stands forever.' And this is the word that was preached to you" (1 Peter 1:23-25).

ATTEMPTS TO KILL THE SEED

Throughout history there have been several efforts to kill or inhibit the Seed. One of these was during the reigns of Decius (249-251) and Diocletian (284-305). These Roman emperors decreed that to possess the Christian scriptures would be a capital offense. (This accounts for the fact that most of the large manuscripts that now exist are after the fourth century.) The Romans knew that to destroy the church they would have to destroy the Seed that produced it.[1] Many church leaders were tortured to reveal the hiding places of the Word. A Christian called Felix responded to his torturers, "It is better that I should be burnt myself, rather than the scriptures."[2]

Was the Seed destroyed? No! In fact, when Constantine later commissioned Eusebius to produce copies of the scriptures, out from the catacombs, caves, closets and other hiding places came the precious Word! The glory of Rome and its emperors are gone but the Seed remains.

Can you imagine chaining Bibles to pulpits so that they could only be read in the church buildings? That is how the medieval church tried to limit the use of Scriptures. Bibles were scarce and very expensive in those days because manuscripts had to be copied by hand. It would take the ordinary working man seven years to pay for one copy! Many times a church would own only one copy and sometimes just a portion of the Scriptures. The church leaders did not want the Bible stolen and then read by the people. The common man could not understand what the Bible said anyway, they reasoned.[3]

But there was one man who reasoned differently. William Tyndale said that before long the plow boy would know more Scripture than the clergy did. He set out to translate the Word amid persecution so severe that he was forced to flee to the Continent from England. His printed New Testaments were smuggled back to England in bales of fabric. He tirelessly kept at his task until a friend betrayed him. He was imprisoned and on October 6, 1536, burned at the stake, where he is said to have cried, "Lord, open the King of England's eyes!"

Ironically in the next century, the English crown gave approval to such Bible translations as Cloverdale's, the Great Bible, the Bishops' Bible and the King James Version of 1611. Interestingly, parts of our English Old Testament and all of our New Testament go back to Tyndale's efforts more than any other translator. About 92% of Tyndale's New Testament is carried over in the King James Version.[4]

In the 18th century it was Voltaire who led the "modernistic" skeptics to reject the authority of the Seed. He boasted he would be the one Frenchman to destroy the Christianity that twelve ignorant fishermen established. He did not succeed. In fact, after his death the Geneva Bible Society purchased his home to store Bibles for distribution![5]

Persecution against God's Word is not new nor has it ceased. Enemies of the Bible from Diocletian in the third century to Madeline Murray O'Hare in the twentieth century have tried to fight its distribution and eliminate its use. They have burned it, banned it and blasphemed it. But their efforts have failed. No book has been read, copied, memorized, cherished and defended more than the Bible. And so it will continue.

TRANSLATIONS—IT'S GREEK TO ME! (AND ARAMAIC AND HEBREW. . .)

It is remarkable to realize that our Bible has not only survived tremendous persecution but has also survived the test of time without losing its message. Through thousands of years, through thousands of hands, through translations and even some mistranslations, the Word has come to us and remained. Does that not say to you that God wants us to have his Word here and now?

Today men have translated the Bible in whole or in part into more than 1,739 languages.[6] But it was first written in just three—Hebrew, Aramaic and Greek. The Old Testament was probably first translated into Greek in the third century B.C. in what is referred to as the Septuagint (LXX). The Greek-speaking Jews used the Septuagint in the time of Jesus. Around A.D. 404 Jerome translated both Old and New Testaments into Latin and this translation was called the Vulgate (from vulgar or common language of the people).

Probably the first translation of the entire Bible into English was the work of John Wyclif in 1382. Wyclif's manuscripts were written by hand (Johannes Gutenburg's printing press was not invented until 1453) so they were quite expensive. Finally opposition against Wyclif and his translators was so strong that Bishop Arundel ordered the Holy Scriptures should not be translated into any language.

As the result of the Renaissance and the Reformation, men yearned to know truth and they wanted to read the Bible for themselves. Flowing through the work of Tyndale and other brave men and women throughout the centuries, many translations have been made. To date we now have 75 translations in contemporary English[8] No perfect translation exists because men, who do the translating, are not infallible. God has seen to it that His Word is available to us to provide us with "everything we need for life and godliness" (2 Peter 1:3).

To truly appreciate the job of the translator, consider these facts:

1. In 1516 Erasmus had only six manuscripts when he translated and printed the first Greek New Testament.

2. No original copies exist today.

3. Thousands of copies were produced and copied by hand repeatedly over a period of 1,600 years.

4. Of all the existing partial and complete New Testament manuscripts—over five thousand in Greek and thousands in Latin—no two anywhere are exactly alike![9]

How would you like to sift through all those manuscripts to find the Truth? It should make us grateful to those translators before us! It is incredible that the efforts of so many different individuals, living in such diverse geographic areas, under such simple conditions, and separated by centuries, should form the book that is the best loved, best known and greatest in the world!

The word Bible comes from the Greek BIBLION meaning "the book." Certainly "the book" is in a class all by itself. What other book has proved itself by surviving thousands of years to this day? Where does one find the unity or teachings or literary genius that surpasses this book? What other book has borne the onslaught of criticism from skeptics and the persecution of disbelievers? Who can deny the divine intervention of history in the fulfillment of biblical prophecy? In what other ancient book do biblical scholarship and archeological discoveries continue to point to its historical reliability? Only one—"the book," the Bible, "God-breathed" Word of God, his Ever Viable Seed.

PUTTING THE SEED IN OUR HEARTS

After the history of God's Word comes alive for us, it makes us appreciate it more fully. Each page has been bought with the blood, sweat and tears of brave men and women over thousands of years through the grace of the Lord. How can we best open the pages and apply those words to our lives today?

There are some ways NOT to study God's Word. The "close-your-eyes-open-the-Bible-and-point-to-God's-message-for-me-today" technique is not truly beneficial. We might gain a momentary flash of insight or blessing but lasting benefits do not come this way. Neither is the "spiritual smorgasbord"—choosing a verse from here and there and trying to make a well-balanced spiritual diet! And the plodding, inflexible one chapter a day through the Bible for the next 1,189 days (there are that many chapters) could easily bog one down.

God gave us His Word in almost every available form of written communication: narrative history, laws, genealogies, chronicles, poetry, proverbs, prophecies, riddles, biographies, parables, sermons, letters and apocalypses. With all these different forms, it is a shame to study it in a dull, overly methodical way.

What is our purpose in studying the Bible anyway? Is it only to know about God? Or is it to also KNOW God? Are we not to try to understand Him and His plan for us in our lives? When we approach the Word with expectation and humility, we seek a closer relationship with God.

Let us look at various ways we can correctly handle the word of truth (2 Timothy 2:15).

THE BASIC ABC's

It is good to remember the ABC principle as we approach the Bible: A—ACCURACY, B—BACKGROUND, and C—COMMON SENSE.

A—ACCURACY. In interpreting a scripture, we should make sure that all people, places and things are defined accurately. For instance, in the Word there are several Herods, four Johns, three Jameses and ten different Simons! It is especially important to define words that have changed meaning over the years.

B—BACKGROUND. Before we interpret a passage, we should make sure we understand its setting and background. You can prove almost anything by the Bible if you take it out of context! Sometimes it is wise to run cross references to get the whole picture. For a start, ask these questions:

1. What is the main idea of the book (or verse or chapter)?
2. Who wrote it?
3. To whom was it written?
4. Where was it written?
5. When was it written?
6. Why was it written?
7. What was the message for the people in that day?
8. What is the message for us today?

C—COMMON SENSE. Use your common sense in reading the Bible. Look for the clear meaning rather than some mysterious symbolic interpretation. Do not force some meaning into some passage that is not there. Some verses lend themselves to symbolic or figurative language. Do not let the difficult verses in God's Word discourage you. Live by what you do understand. Mark Twain once quipped, "It isn't what I don't understand in the Bible that bothers me, but what I do understand!"[10]

Where does one begin in his study? I believe our first goal should be to read the Bible through at least once before we tackle detailed studies of any kind. How else can we get the whole picture if we dwell on the New Testament or certain parts of the Old? This overview should be a cursory one, just like a geologist studying a mountain. First he should get the "wide-screen" view—perhaps an aerial photo—before he starts picking away at the rocks. As T.C. Hammond advised new converts, "Read the Bible in great dollops!"[11]

Continually reading the Bible in great dollops, however, would allow one to miss jewels found inside the mountian. The geologist must get the overview but then he zeroes in and focuses all his attention on a small square foot area. Searching for clues to the past, he carefully examines stone by stone. So it is with our Bible study.

After we read the entire Bible, we are ready to focus on an area of need or interest to us. It is helpful to begin a spiritual journal, containing questions, answers and insights. Date your entries to see how faithful your study truly is. You might even put a prayer list in the back and note how these prayers are answered. Keep a pen or highlighter handy for marking scriptures that are important to you. Let us look at the variety of ways to approach the "mountain."

METHODS TO STUDY THE BIBLE

1. BOOK STUDY. It is generally best to make an outline of the book. Sometimes it is helpful to start with a simpler one like the one of the Gospels, Acts, Psalms, or Proverbs. Revelation is definitely a meatier choice for concentrated study!

2. CHAPTER ANALYSIS. Concentrating on single chapters and extracting every ounce of goodness from them can prove profitable. Some favorites are Proverbs 31, 1 Corinthians 13 and Hebrews 11. You might discover another one that will become your personal favorite.

3. SUBJECT OR TOPICAL STUDY. This involves studying one topic in depth. For instance, you might study the subject of the "church." Besides learning the original language definitions, you could run references on the various names for the church found in the New Testament such as The Way, church of Christ, church of God, royal priesthood, peculiar people, etc. Included in this study might be the church's purpose, organization, and requirements for membership. This method of study can be quite extensive if you wish. Other topics might be prayer, mercy, judgement, and prophecy.

4. VERSE ANALYSIS. Although verses must be taken in their overall context to derive their true meaning, sometimes one or a few have so much "meat" they should be isolated for study. Take, for example, the works of the flesh in Galatians 5:19-21 and the fruit of the Spirit in Galatians 5:22-23. This method is especially helpful for "dissecting" difficult verses.

5. CHARACTER STUDY. I believe this is one of our favorite studies because it shows us how human those Bible people really were. Walking in their dusty sandals by feeling and thinking like they did, we might discover that we might not have acted much better than they did! We also see how incredible their faith really was. (How would YOU like to be thrown to the lions or in a fiery furnace?) Besides noting their family background, education, character traits, friends, and walk with God, we could ask, "What can I learn from this character's life that will help me?"

6. JESUS' LIFE AND TEACHINGS. Many Bible students find that reading some Scriptures about Jesus every day allows His life and teachings to permeate their hearts. For the study of Jesus' works, it would be beneficial to have a harmony of the Gospels to correlate the details of the events.

7. JESUS' PARABLES. We single out the parables of Jesus because of their great teaching value. Especially important in this study would be an understanding of the background preceding the parables and a cautious attitude toward drawing too many interpretations from these simple stories. Many times Jesus provided His own interpretation.

8. PSALM STUDY. A study of this Hebrew poetry can be enlightening. When the information is given, pay attention to who the writer was and why he might have written the psalm. For instance, David wrote Psalm 51 after Nathan the prophet

had condemned his sin with Bathsheba. This gives us an extra dimension of David's character.

9. PROVERBS STUDY. Each proverb could provide a "mini-study" in itself! The book is so chock full of practical goodies for living that it is often begun as a first study after the entire Bible has been read. Its thirty-one chapters can be easily read a chapter a day for a month.

10. PROPHECY STUDY. A real faith builder, a study of the prophecies of God's Word and their fulfillment provides some of the unity that binds the Bible together. The omnipotent, omniscient scope of God's plan is seen in the fulfillment of the smallest details of the birth and death of Christ, the establishment of the church, and other events.

11. WORD STUDY. Choose a word, study its original language definition, then find all the references in which it is found. You might be surprised at the different shades of meaning one word can have. Examples include: holy, love, grace, repent, faith, peace, propitiation, reconciliation, sanctification.

12. ROOT STUDY. Not to be confused with "Word Study," the root study traces relationships between scriptures, often between the Old and New Testament. For example, a study could be made of the atoning death of Christ spoken about in Hebrews compared and contrasted to the sacrificial lamb of the Old Law. This method is excellent for tying together concepts and for showing how unified God's Word truly is.[12]

As you can see, these study methods are alike in some ways; yet each is a distinct attempt to focus on the Bible in unique perspectives from different levels. The same book can be understood by the simple and can baffle the intellectual! It is a book for all ages for all seasons for all men.

For example, the same story—Jonah—can be applied differently at various levels. The preschooler could be taught obedience. The school-ager could be encouraged to have the courage to speak up for right. The importance of missionary efforts could be stressed to teens and adults. So God's timeless message has something to say to everyone.

So as the geologist starts carefully digging to find his hidden gem, so let us start digging!

There is a story from ancient Greece of a rich farmer who was dying. On his deathbed he told his two sons, "My treasure—your inheritance—is buried in my fields. If you would be wealthy, go dig for it."

When the old man died, the boys eagerly set out to discover what they supposed to be gold and jewels in an iron chest, buried somewhere in the field. With mattocks and spades, they dug to depths that no plow had ever reached. With endurance and perserverance they turned over the soil of every field, but with no luck.

Their search was finally abandoned in spring with the sowing of the crops. Then came summer and the harvest. What a harvest it was! It brought forth riches that only digging so deeply could bring. The plan of the father had worked.[13]

We too have inherited a treasure that has been passed down through many generations. It is buried not in a field but in a book. To discover its gems, we must diligently dig but it is certainly worth digging for. The deeper we dig the more we can discover. Each turn of the spade reveals a new thought, a fresh gem. This precious heirloom is, of course, the Bible. How deep are we digging?

WHO ME—MEMORIZE?

You can say the word "memorization" and people start saying how they can hardly remember any one's name, much less a Bible verse. Or memory work is just for kids. Or simply that their brain cells are all used up! (Actually, it is estimated that the average human mind has 12 billion brain cells but only about 10% of that potential is ever used!) God made our brains and He can help us remember his Word. So it is time for us to get those brain gears cranking for even a rusty machine works better if it is oiled and used. Some people claim they can remember names better after they begin a Bible memory program!

> I know the latest recipes by heart;
> I can tell all the movie stars apart;
> I know all the new programs on TV;
> I know all the ball players from a to z;
> I know every big-wig in this town;
> I know the bargain prices up and down.
> But with Scripture, I am not reliable;
> I just can't seem to remember the Bible.
>
> Unknown Author

Today in our busy fast-moving society, we are told to put everything down on paper to remember it and perhaps this has become our crutch. Before the use of handy writing materials, man was forced to remember what he heard if he wanted to recall something from the past. Perhaps memorizing is a lost art today. It is time to get this art revived![14]

Dean and Grace Merrill tell of their family scripture memory system in their book TOGETHER AT HOME. Their idea came from Dean's childhood. When he was about four, his parents started putting verses on 3x5 cards. The verse was written on one side, the reference on the other and the cards were stored in a recipe box. When he learned to write, he wrote the verses himself. Not only does this aid the memory process but it provides a record of a child's progressive handwriting.

A verse a week was added for the next twelve years. At the end of that time Dean had a bulging file box and more than 600 verses "fixed" in his mind! The key was review. Several times a week his mother would move a stiff marker through the verses as Dean would recite each verse. Have the Scriptures "stuck" after more than twenty-five years? Yes, the majority have!

Some families find a memory verse notebook helpful. Verses can be illustrated by hand or pictures from books and magazines. Due to frequent use, loose-leaf paper holes might be reinforced if used for this purpose.

We must not become discouraged if we or our children did not begin memorizing Scripture when we were four years old. Let us begin now! At the beginning it could be a family project. Then as interest and ages differ, family members could pick their own verses for their own needs.

If you are all learning the same verse, it might be fun to go "Round Robin," saying just two words to a person. The verse can be learned in several rounds by starting with different people each time.

An initial goal might be to learn one verse from each of the sixty-six books (some will take more searching than others). One family periodically has a contest to see who can remember a verse from each book of the Bible.

You can pick your own verses to memorize or take them from Bible School lessons. Sometimes a specific need makes a certain verse more timely. The verse should be understood with difficult terms explained to make memorization more meaningful. One four-year old was certain his new memory verse in Isaiah 53:6 was "All we like sheep have gone to Australia!"

With Scripture memory it is a matter of "use it or lose it." Constant review makes the difference. No matter what method we use, let us begin now to "fix" God's Word in our hearts and minds.

Why should we "fix"God's Word in our hearts permanently? I cannot say it better than the Psalmist:

> How can a young man keep his way pure? By living according to your word. I seek you with all my heart; do not let me stray from your commands. I have hidden your Word in my heart that I might not sin against you. Praise be to you, O LORD; teach me your decrees. With my lips I recount all the laws that come from your mouth. I rejoice in following your statutes as one rejoices in great riches. I meditate on your precepts and consider your ways. I delight in your decrees; I will not neglect your word (Psalms 119:9-16).

Through centuries of turmoil and persecution, our Bible has survived and is well and alive today! The Bible is truly the Ever Viable Seed. The Psalmist again described the Seed best:

> The law of the LORD is perfect, reviving the soul. The statutes of the LORD are trustworthy, making wise the simple. The precepts of the LORD are right, giving joy to the heart. The commands of the LORD are radiant, giving light to the eyes. The fear of the LORD is pure, enduring forever. The ordinances of the LORD are sure and altogether righteous. They are

more precious than gold, than much pure gold; they are sweeter than honey, than honey from the comb. By them is your servant warned; in keeping them there is great reward (Psalms 19:7-11).

CHAPTER 6
THE EVER VIABLE SEED
Digging Deeper

1. Briefly describe how the Bible was transmitted to us today.

2. Why should we be thankful to have easy access to the Bible today compared to other times in history?

3. Find out more about the efforts of Voltaire, the Frenchman who said he would destroy the Christianity that twelve ignorant fisherman sought to establish.

4. Name some important people who helped translate the Bible into the language of the common people.

5. How many original manuscripts exist today? Approximately when was the last original written?

6. Identify some inefficient ways to study the Bible.

7. Name some forms of written communication that are found in the Bible.

8. What is the ABC principle of Bible study and why is it important to put into practice?

9. Why is it not best to continue to read the Bible in "great dollops"?

10. How can we develop more interest in memorizing the Bible?

CHAPTER SEVEN

A Time to Sow

"There is a time for everything, and a season for every activity under heaven:...a time to plant and a time to uproot..." (Ecclesiastes 3:1-2)

Knowing the best time to sow is of utmost importance to the farmer for the maximum yield of his crop. Some farmers would not dare drop a seed in the ground without consulting their trusty Farmer's Almanac. They believed their almanac had just the right planting times for their particular locale. Other farmers time their planting by the "fruit tree calendar." The hardy vegetables like parsnips, onions and beets are planted when the peach and pear trees are in bloom. When apple blossoms appear, the tender varieties like cucumbers, melons, and corn are sown.

Timing is also important in planting the Seed spiritually. There will be times when our teaching will be absorbed and other times when it will be ignored, or at least less enthusiastically accepted. Our job is to find those times when our children are more teachable and reachable and utilize them to their fullest. It sometimes takes a little planning to make these times happen.

What did God tell Moses about when to teach children? Before we seek that answer, let us first put ourselves in the historical sandals of the hearers of this message. Moses was reviewing God's laws with the Israelites, who were just on the brink of Canaan. God wanted to warn them of this land where the worship of false gods was rampant. So Moses talks essentially to parents—first, that their dedication to God must be real; and second, that they must diligently teach their children God's commands. For spiritual survival, no passive, half-hearted approach in Canaan would work!

Hear, O Israel: The LORD our God, the LORD is one. Love the LORD your God with all your heart and with all your soul and with all your strength. These commandments that I give you today are to be upon your hearts. Impress them on your children. TALK ABOUT THEM WHEN YOU SIT

AT HOME AND WHEN YOU WALK ALONG THE ROAD, WHEN YOU LIE DOWN AND WHEN YOU GET UP (Emphasis mine. NE). Tie them as symbols on your hands and bind them on your foreheads. Write them on the doorframes of your houses and on your gates (Deuteronomy 6:4-9).

It is interesting that this passage, called the SHEMA, is considered the most important of Jewish prayers. In it we see how the dedicated Jew took these commands literally by putting tefillin or phylacteries on his arm and head and placing a mezzuzah on his doorpost. Some Jews still do this today.

Devout Jewish parents take the teaching command literally today too. In addition to being taught at home, Jewish children either attend special religion classes in addition to public schools or they attend special schools. They study the Bible, Hebrew language, the Jewish prayerbook, selections from the Midrash, Talmud, Bible commentaries and contemporary history of the Jewish people.[1]

Let us isolate the times in Deuteronomy 6:4-9 that God referred to teaching children—" . . .when you sit. . .when you walk. . .when you lie down. . .when you get up." That pretty well covers all bases. We are so afraid we will overdo it that we are more likely to softpeddle spiritual things with our kids. This scripture sounds more akin to brainwashing in its best sense!

In commenting on this passage, David Lipscomb said:

> . . .*That meant every servant of God was to be a Bible teacher; his house was to be a Bible house; his home, a Bible home; and his eyes and hands, Bible eyes and hands. The Bible was to be taught by all servants of God, at all times, in all places, to all their children.*[2]

Someone might say, "Oh, that was fine for them! In their agricultural society, parents and children worked side by side and that might have worked. Today it's vastly different. Do you know how much I see my kid, much less teach him?"

It is true that our society is a far cry from the tents of the Hebrew culture. But has our responsibility changed because the times have changed? Are we still not accountable for teaching our children when we can, as often as we can, wherever we can?

I think God wanted our spiritual training to flow through the natural setting of our homes. As Mary White says, "Talking of spiritual things should be vital, but not stilted; natural, but not frivolous; frequent, but not tedious."[3] This means no preaching or lectures, but rather spontaneous and planned times when our children are best able to digest the milk—and then the meat—of the Word. This might occur when sitting or walking or lying down or getting up.

More likely, in our hurry-scurry society, we run instead of walk where we are going and feel that there is no time for talking, much less for teaching. If we do stop long enough to sit, it is usually in front of a TV!

Let us use the "magic moments" (and those not quite so magic) and make them count as quality teaching time for God.

MAKING AND TAKING THE TIME TO PLANT

Boswell, a biographer of Samuel Johnson, often told about the day his dad had taken him fishing. It had meant so much to him as a young lad. A curious researcher checked Boswell's father's diary to see how his father had recorded this particular event. There opposite the date was penned, "Gone fishing today with my son; a day wasted."[4]

Do we feel like time spent with our children is wasted? There are things we had rather do, even things that we need to do, that demand our attention. Are they really more important than our children? Sometimes it is the time we think we "waste" with our kids that means so much to them.

TO MY GROWN-UP SONS

My hands were busy through the day
I didn't have much time to play
The little games you asked me to
I didn't have much time for you.

I'd wash your clothes, I'd sew and cook
But when you'd bring your picture book
And ask me please to share your fun
I'd say, "A little later, son."

I'd tuck you in all safe at night
And hear your prayers, turn out the light
Then tiptoe softly to the door
I wish I'd stayed a minute more.

For life is short, the years rush past
A little boy grows up so fast
No longer is he at your side
His precious secrets to confide.

The picture books are put away
There are no more games to play
No goodnight kiss, no prayers to hear·
That all belongs to yesteryear.

My hands once busy now lie still
The days are long and hard to fill
I wish I might go back and do
The little things you asked me to.

Anonymous

55

Before we can plant God's seed in our children's hearts, we must take the time to do it. We often hear the cry, "It isn't the quantity of time we spend with our children that counts but the quality of time." Certainly, quality is important. But it is difficult to spend quality time without making some quantity of time to do it!

UTILIZING THE TEACHABLE MOMENT

Sometimes prime teaching opportunities come our way if we only have our eyes open to see them. Sometimes a moment might be used more effectively than a 30-minute lecture. Here are examples of those "teachable moments," those serendipitous times when spiritual truths can be discovered.

1. CHILDREN'S QUESTIONS: In spite of sometimes being a nuisance, many questions come straight from a child's innate curiosity and should not be brushed aside. Questions about spiritual matters serve as an opportunity for further instruction.

Some children's queries evolve as humorous as they are thought-provoking. For example, "If God made everyone in his own image, how come some people are ugly?" or "If we're here on earth to serve others, what are the others supposed to do?" or "If the man the Samaritan helped was half-dead, which half was dead?" But when a child asks a question, we know at least he has been thinking! Then is the time to answer that probing mind—he might never be that primed for that particular answer for a long while, if ever!

However, sometimes we might have to wait for a more appropriate time for our explanations. I remember being poked in the ribs several Sundays when both our young children asked, "Can I have some grape juice and crackers?" To them, the Lord's Supper was a snack break in a long service. Clearly, the time and place to explain all this was not during the Lord's Supper. I finally remembered to explain it after services when it was fresh in our minds.

It is good for children to know that their parents do not know everything but they can find an answer somewhere, especially from God's Word. A well-chosen book can introduce delicate subjects like sex or death appropriately. Books do not take the place of our explanations but they make them easier! Sometimes a book can complete a partial understanding of a subject.

2. FEARS. Fears are a part of most, if not all, children's lives. They present a challenge and opportunity for us to show God's care for His children and our child in particular.

In her book GROWING TOGETHER, Mary White gives an example of how she and her husband helped their 10-year old daughter through a period of fearfulness. She feared death, the dark, separation from her parents, new situations, and any possible disaster. She questioned her hope of heaven, God's love for her, and the truth of the Bible.

As she went to bed every night, her parents put on tape recorded Christian music and scripture that saturated her mind as she drifted off to sleep. This diversion from her fears made it possible for her to focus on the Lord. After several weeks of prayer and this nighttime focusing, the daughter became confident again in God and in herself.

This particular process might not work for every child with one or more fears but it does show the power of God's Word and prayer to anchor faith and overcome fear, even in a child.

3. BRUISED KNEES AND BRUISED EGOS. Hurts, whether they are large or small, physical or emotional, need to be soothed. Parents are the mirrors of God's great concern for all his children when they are hurt. Through our love, we can show that we care and God cares.

We all appreciate sympathy when we are physically hurt. Somehow a hurt feels better when a bandaid is lovingly applied, whether needed or not! A hug, a kiss, a love pat—all show a little T.L.C.

Bruised egos are harder to mend and take more than a loving touch and a bandaid. The ego is in a delicate balance especially during the topsy-turvy world of the teen. Confidence must be built on God and this faith should extend to everyday happenings. Knowing that God will lead us through the emotional small dips in the road as well as the deep valleys will help us handle both better when they come. If we help with the "scratches" of the schoolage child, the teenager will come to us with his larger "wounds."

Sharing a personal similar incident might help him see that he is not alone. This can be especially effective in a family devotional situation where older members share their experiences.

Studying the lives of young people in the Bible like Daniel, David, Esther and Joseph can also be beneficial. By facing challenges and overcoming them courageously, these Bible characters serve as role models to emulate.

4. NATURE. Sometimes we feel we just have to get away for a weekend or week or two before we can truly enjoy the beauty of God's creation. But I think God saw the magnitude of the moment—"Be still, and know that I am God;" (Psalms 46:10). Even a few moments of quiet with nature can teach a lot.

Think how the Master Teacher taught God's Truth to His childlike listeners. Often Jesus used nature as His illustration—lilies of the field, birds, foxes, mustard seed, fruit. Many times His listeners had the panorama of nature before them as He spoke. He used nature as a familiar visual aid for teaching.

We are fortunate to have David's recorded inspirational thoughts about nature in the Psalms. Perhaps playing his harp while he tended his sheep, David would look up into the sky and think:

The heavens declare the glory of God; the skies proclaim the work of his hands. Day after day they pour forth speech; night after night they display knowledge. There is no speech or language where their voice is not heard (Psalm 19:1-3).

What better way to bring the written Word alive to our children than through God's nature! Here are a few ideas that perhaps can do just that.

—Proverbs 6:6-8. Go find an anthill. Put out some big crumbs and see how the ants manage.

—Job 38-41. List the ways nature is exalted. Take the kids to a wildlife sanctuary or the ocean. Try to count the stars at night.

—Psalm 33:6-7; Psalm 65:5-13; Psalm 104; Proverbs 30:24-31. Draw various examples of God's creation. Visit a zoo or a conservatory.

—Mark 4:1-9. Explain the Parable of the Sower. Let the family find each of the kinds of soils in their yard. Tell what each soil represents from the parable. Start a mini-garden in a milk carton.

Paul said, "For since the creation of the world God's invisible qualities—His eternal power and divine nature—have been clearly seen, being understood from what has been made so that men are without excuse" (Romans 1:20). God has stamped His unique indelible mark, His "designer label" on all the universe. Let us make God clear to our children through His creation for there are many who try to muddy His divinity and deny His existence.

UTILIZING THE PLANNED MOMENTS

I call these moments "planned," yet we might question how planned some of these activities might be! At least they are regular occurrences in most households! These suggestions are not meant to fill every minute of these times in a tedious fashion but rather be interspersed in a fun-loving spirit.

1. MEALTIME. Throughout history family mealtimes have meant more than just sharing a common meal. They were an avenue to impart values to growing children—and that does not just mean table manners! To the Jews, meals held special significance, especially during feasts and celebrations. It is significant that Jesus ate the Passover meal with His disciples and thereby instituted the Lord's Supper before His imminent death. After His resurrection He chose to eat with them again to further instruct them.

One reason given for the breakdown of Japanese families during their stay in U.S. internment camps during World War II was the loss of the family table and kitchen. Children ate with children while adults ate with adults; only when they slept were they all together. They were given little time to be together and communicate.[5]

Today family mealtimes together are falling on hard times. With school activities, varying work schedules and that other dinner guest—TV, getting everyone to sit down together for a meal is depressingly harder to do. But mealtime can be more meaningful. It might take a little juggling of schedules but the benefits far outweigh any inconvenience. The following hints might help.

—Turn off the TV. An occasional meal in front of the boob tube will not hurt, but a constant diet of meals a la TV makes communication between family members difficult, if not impossible.

—Be interested and listen to others. Ask questions to find out what everyone did that day. Occasionally get the conversational ball rolling by drawing from a question box or topics bowl to introduce items the family would like to duscuss. Or how about religious questions to debate?

—Introduce spiritual teaching. Thanking God for the food is a good start. Make sure to vary the blessing to prevent monotone ritual. Some families find after dinner or breakfast devotions or Scripture readings fit the bill in their homes. Others learn verses together during the preparation of their meals. Many interject teaching (disguised of course!) through the conversation. Such leads as "Cindy called my best friend 'Blubberface' and I didn'ʇ know what to do" or "I told my science teacher that the world was made by God and everyone laughed" provide ample opportunity for teaching in a conversational setting.

How about meals in a restaurant? That seemingly never-ending wait between ordering and having our hot food placed before us can be used to creatively teach our children. Instead of poking fun at the fat man two booths over or complaining about the slow service, could not we use the time differently? Some alternatives: silently pray for the people in the restaurant, take in Bible coloring books for the younger set, or hold a short Bible bee.

Dean and Grace Merrill in TOGETHER AT HOME describe the time in a pizza parlor that they had their children learn Colossians 3:23: "Whatever you do, work at it with all your heart, as working for the Lord, not for men." The family then observed their waitress to see what kind of attitude she portrayed. The waitress never knew it but she passed with flying colors! The kids learned the verse and a graphic illustration of its meaning (and stayed out of trouble until food arrived).

2. BEDTIME. Bedtimes can be pretty wild and wooly around some households so it is wise to "plan backwards" to allow enough time for all that needs to be done. If the kiddos have a 9:00 in-bed-and-no-other-wishes-granted time, then count back to 8:30 or 8:00 for baths and devotional/quiet talk time. Gathering around a Bible story book or family Bible provides a quieting end to the day. Some families split their devotion times to accomodate different ages. Other families part with a family prayer to spend the last minutes of the day in their devotional reading.

One busy preacher, a father of six, who is frequently away, schedules his children's bedtimes at half hour intervals so he can talk to each one of his children, and pray with them individually. Even after children feel too old to be tucked in, they enjoy the quiet of bedtime to talk and empty the frustration and joys of the day on a sympathizing ear. It is also a good time to pray about upcoming games, tests or dates.

3. VACATIONS AND TRIPS. When some people go on a vacation trip they develop the "Jonah complex"—"If I get far enough away, God won't see me!" The only Bible they see is the one left in the motel by the Gideons and the only church building they view is the one they whiz by on the way to the beach!

God does not have to be left behind. Utilizing this time for spiritual learning that is enjoyable can also prevent squabbles in the back seat. Here are some activities that might work with your family.

—Memorize Scripture and discuss what it means. One family learned Philippians 4:8 as they hiked the three-mile trail around a beautiful lake. The verse became a chant as each person took an adjective, "...whatsoever things are TRUE, whatsoever things are HONEST, whatsoever things are JUST..." etc. They repeated it until they had it down pat. They call it their "Hiking Scripture."

—Read a short Bible book or chapter and explore how you might put it into practice on your vacation.

—Read a religious book, fiction or nonfiction. Sometimes reading makes long hours in the car pass more quickly.

—Take along cassette tapes of hymns, spiritual songs and Bible stories. Or record your own Bible stories beforehand and ask questions afterwards. Or let the kids do a "You are There" interview with a famous Bible character.

—Stick in some Bible workbooks, sticker and activity books with crossword puzzles and hidden words. Your Christian bookstore might even carry religious travel fun books.

—Sing gospel songs. Besides being relaxing, this is great practice for everyone, even if all some in the family can do is make a "joyful noise"!

—Distribute gospel tracts everywhere you stop. Who knows but that someone will find one and be won to Christ. Even the youngest child can do this.

—Some guessing games lend themselves well for travel. It is even fun to make up your own. Here are a few:

a. BIBLE WHO AM I—Describe a Bible character. The first one to corrently guess gets to describe another character.

b. BIBLE A B C—Someone calls out a letter of the alphabet and each person guesses as many Bible persons or places as he can with that letter. The one who names the most is the winner.

c. IS IT?—Someone says a letter of the alphabet. Each person must ask an "identity question" to which the first person must answer. Example: "J." "Is it the Son of God?" "No, it is not Jesus." "Is it the father of Joseph?" "No, it is not Jacob." "Is it the disciple that betrayed Jesus?" "Yes, it is Judas." Then the person who guessed correctly gets to choose the next name.

d. BIBLE COLORS—Think of a Bible expression using color, such as white as snow, red like crimson, green pastures, sins be as scarlet, a seller of purple, or

Joseph's coat of many colors.

e. ADD A BIBLE WORD—Say a word; then add a word beginning with last letter of the word before. Example: JesuS, StepheN, NicodemuS. Divide by O.T. and N.T. to add more challenge for older children.

f. AND THEN—Start a Bible story, stop in the middle and then let another person continue.

g. GOING TO JERICHO—This is good for memory as well as a knowledge of Bible people and things. One person says, "I'm going to Jericho and I'm taking an Ark" or any other Bible person or thing that starts with A. The next person must remember that plus add a word starting with B and so on. The last one who can stay in without forgetting is the winner.

—Show an interest in the people you meet. With the emphasis on "strangers and their dangers," we have found it easier to be more aloof. But under certain circumstances we can be an example in friendliness to our children to those we do not know.

—Thank God for a safe arrival home. It is said that Marshall Keeble, after returning home from a gospel meeting, would always kneel in prayer and thank God for a safe trip.

4. HOLIDAYS. With some creativity and planning, we can make the holidays special (and teach our children too!) without fitting into the world's materialistic mold.

—LABOR DAY. Contrary to popular belief, God gave man work so he would be happier. Even in his beautiful garden paradise, Adam was told to name all living creatures (Genesis 2:19-20) and to take care of the garden (Genesis 2:15). Since then man has worked or refused to!

Top cupcakes or a cake with different toys, symbolic of various occupations. Pray with your children about choosing an occupation that will utilize their talents and glorify God (1 Corinthians 10:31).

—HALLOWEEN. Who says the kids always have to be "treated" on Halloween? One family switched tradition by making Halloween cookies together and delivering them to friends.

Prepare an orange meal (orange salad, spaghetti, pumpkin pie, etc.) and carve a jack-o-lantern together. After lighting it, turn off all other lights and tell of times you have been afraid. Think of Bible characters who feared something and how they overcame their fears. Then say (and memorize), "The Lord is my light and my salvation—whom shall I fear. . ." (Psalm 27:1).

Arrange a mask centerpiece and think about the "masks" we wear everyday. Discuss the Pharisees, the masks they wore, and the reason Jesus called them hypocrites. Do we fool people or, more importantly, God, with our masks?

Instead of sweet treats, some families give out pencils, wrapped with simplified gospel tracts for children.

—KID'S DAY. Actually there are two possible dates for honoring our children—September 23 (Kiwanis International) and the second Sunday of June. What would our children say if we honored them by feeding them breakfast in bed, baking their favorite dessert, or taking them on an outing? It would be a good time to remind them how Jesus loved the children (Matthew 18:1-5; Mark 10:13-16; Luke 18:15-17). What better time to show our children how special they are to us!

—THANKSGIVING. Start a "Family Thanksgiving Book" by collecting photographs or magazine pictures that show the many things for which the family is thankful.

Begin a family project of giving up something (dessert one night? meat one night?) to give the money to someone in need.

Write thank you letters to the minister, elders, deacons, missionaries and other church leaders for their hard work.

Reenact the story of Jesus and the ten lepers. (Three actors can complete the cast if that is all you have.)

On a bulletin board or blackboard write an acrostic for THANKSGIVING (Toys, Hamburgers, etc.) and then pray to God, thanking him for each of those things.

Find some thanksgiving prayers in the Bible and tell the circumstances surrounding each. For example, there was Moses' song after crossing the Red Sea (Exodus 15:1-18) or Mary's song during her visit to Elizabeth (Luke 1:46-55).

—CHRISTMAS. Stress the giving of this season instead of the getting. Ask, "What are you giving for Christmas?" Some families encourage this attitude by letting each giver take his gift to the recipient personally and then sit beside him while he opens it. Contrast this to the 15 minute scramble of arms, wrapping paper and the disappointed whine, "Is this ALL I get?"

Make Christmas cookies and/or favors and deliver them to the sick, shut-ins and the elderly in nursing homes.

Shop with your child to select a new toy especially for some less fortunate child and deliver it anonymously.

—VALENTINE'S DAY. Make a puzzle in the shape of a heart of the traits of LOVE found in 1 Corinthians 13.

Build a "love web." With a red or pink ball of yarn, pass a genuine compliment to a family member at the table or devo circle. "I love you because you are patient with me when we are running late." Go two or three rounds until the yarn is a real web. Ask, "What happens when we pull tight? What happens when we all loosen up? What happens when one of us lets down?" Make the appropriate analogies to working together in the family and in the church.

Hold a Valentine Treasure Hunt (similar to Easter egg hunt) by hiding red hearts and messages or verses about love.

—FATHER'S DAY, MOTHER'S DAY. Have a quiz about the honored parent regarding their personal likes and dislikes—song, dessert, sports, food, movie, scripture, animal. Go around and let each person say what they appreciate most about Mom or Dad. Dicuss some good and not so good parents in the Bible.

—EASTER. When the "Christian world" is focusing its attention on Christ's death, burial and resurrection this one Sunday, it is important for our children to know that evey Sunday should be so honored.

Instead of just candy eggs for an indoor or outdoor Easter egg hunt, include some scripture clues to find the next egg. For example, "You will find the next egg clue under something on Mom and Dad's bed. Jacob slept on a stone instead of it (Genesis 28:11)." At the end of the hunt the surprise treasure could be a hosiery egg with a prize inside.

—NEW YEAR'S DAY. This day is perfect for looking back and looking forward. On a cake or casserole, light candles and lower the lights. Each person could share a blessing in his life for the past year and ask the Lord to help with a spiritual goal in the coming year. After everyone has had a turn, blow out the candles and end with a prayer.

This might be a good time for plotting out future family times together. Get ideas for things the family can do and learn this year. Set some spiritual family goals like "This year we will try to invite a family over twice a month, learn a verse a week together," etc. Make a Family Fun Box and put in suggestions.

Highlight some "Days to Remember" that have special significance to your family. God is still doing some incredible things (and in your family particularly)!

5. CELEBRATIONS. We do not have to have a holiday to celebrate! We can often make up our own reasons for celebrating, which makes it more fun and personal.

—BIRTHDAYS. High on a child's—and everyone else's—list of celebrations is his own birthday. It is the only day in the year when we all feel we have an excuse (or reason!) to be honored. This is a good time to build self-image, whether the child is 6 or 86! Older people enjoy a cake and candles as much as a youngster. Interview the birthday girl or boy on a tape recorder each birthday. The recording will become more priceless each year. Why not add a personal touch by telling the story of his birthday and how God blessed the family with him.

When you learn of a baby being born, it is a prime time to talk to your children about God's plan for sex, appropriate to their ages. Discuss Psalms 127:3-5 and emphasize what a precious blessing children are to their parents. Pray for the new baby and parents too.

—WEDDINGS AND ANNIVERSARIES. After attending a wedding, discuss God's plan for marriage in Ephesians 5:22-33. Be sure to pray for the happy couple. Weddings can serve as springboards for talking about dating, sex, and parenthood as well.

Anniversaries can be more than a night out for Mom and Dad (though that is important!) Haul out the wedding pictures and let the kids giggle at the outdated hair styles and gowns. Tell them about the ceremony. Show them that the love and trust committed to each other then is just as important today. Pray for your children, whether God wills for them to marry or remain single.

—GRADUATION. At these milestones, some families hold a "This is Your Life" review with pictures and slides of the person's life. Important events could be highlighted in scrapbooks. Such backward perspective gives the person added incentive for making and reaching future goals. Spiritual past and future goals should be included, such as the individual's baptism, first song led in front of the congregtion (for boys), or first children's class taught.

—"JUST BECAUSE YOU'RE HOME." Appreciate your children before they head for college or a new life away from home. Honor them with their favorite dinner and a focus on their special qualities and God-given talents. This positive reinforcement is good for young children as well as teenagers.

—SPIRITUAL BIRTHDAYS. It is a happy day when our children obey the gospel! Why not celebrate their spiritual birth as well as their physical birth? Decorate the house, make a birthday cake, and invite friends. A gift could be chosen to go with the spiritual theme. Some parents gave their daughter an Avon key ring. Then everyone was asked to write down, on key-shaped paper, a spiritual thought or verse to be used as keys to the daughter's spiritual growth in the next year. These were shared out loud and then handed over to her.

For those too young to be accountable, a "Susie loves Jesus" party could be planned. This could be held just like a "spiritual birthday" except not at any particular time of the year.

—DEDICATION OF A GIFT. In our affluent society it is easy to believe that what we have belongs wholly to us. To combat this ME-MY-MINE attitude, why not dedicate to God what you receive with a short prayer and/or ceremony. "Lord, we thank you for giving us this new house (or car or piano or sewing machine or electric saw). We know it is really yours and we pray we will use it in your service. In Christ's Name, Amen." This reminder would help us and our children see to whom everything really belongs!

—JOB MOVES OR CHANGES. Our society is a mobile one with more families making major moves every year. But the disruption to the family is still there no matter how frequently it occurs. We can help prepare our children by praying for new friends and easy adjustments to a new school and neighborhood. A look at Bible families and the reasons for their moves and job changes can help show that God sometimes calls his people to make changes but he helps in the process. Some examples are: Noah, Abraham, Jacob, Moses, Ruth, and Esther. God's words to movers include: Genesis 12:1-3; Deuteronomy 1:6-8; Matthew 2:13-15, 19-23.

THE RIGHT TIME

Finding the appropriate time to teach is a challenge to the conscientious Christian parent. There is so much to teach and so little time! But some planning and inspiration can go a long way. To add to Lora Laycock's quip about teaching our young: "KNOW YOUR STUFF! KNOW HIM WHOM YOU ARE STUFFING! KNOW WHEN TO STUFF! KNOW HOW TO STUFF! AND THEN STUFF!"

CHAPTER 7
A TIME TO SOW
Digging Deeper

1. What are the *Midrash* and the *Talmud* and why do devout Jews find them so important to study?

2. What were some "teachable moments" of your own childhood that you remember?

3. Why is it important for parents to listen and try to answer their children's questions? Why should children understand that their parents do not know everything?

4. What are some fears that young children have? How can our example help them overcome their fears?

5. How can "bruised knees and bruised egos" present an opportunity to show our love and God's love?

6. Find scripture references of parables in which Jesus used examples of nature.

7. Can you think of some times when you have felt closer to God through nature?

8. Why has TV been so detrimental to mealtime?

9. How can we teach our children to be friendly to people they meet without getting into compromising situations?

10. Name some ways that time spent together during holidays and celebrations can bring a family together. Think of some examples in your own family.

CHAPTER EIGHT

Preparing the Soil

"Even the best of soil must first be broken before it can become beautiful." Phillip Keller

Before planting the seed, the gardener has to cultivate the ground. Breaking up the soil gives it a chance to breathe. Aerated soil is healthier soil. Seeds have a better chance for survival if they send out their tiny shoots into plowed dirt, free of large stones and clumps of clay. The importance of prepared soil is paramount because it lies at the root of the matter!

Likewise our precious soil—the hearts of our children—needs to be lovingly prepared. Just like we would not go out and sprinkle seed on hard or rocky ground, so we cannot expect to "dump" the Word on our children one day. Preparation needs to begin at birth—even before birth.

A man once said that the child should love God 20 years before he is born. This refers to the important role of parents in devoting themselves and then their child to the Lord. Let us look at a beautiful example of this devotion.

HANNAH GAVE HIM BACK

Any woman who has ever longed for a child can empathize with Hannah. Year after year she was unable to have children and this was especially shameful for a Hebrew. Her husband Elkanah tried to ease her pain—"Don't I mean more to you than ten sons?"—but it just was not the same. Elkanah's other wife Peninnah was not quite so sympathetic. With her own sons and daughters running about, Peninnah taunted Hannah until she cried. We too might shed tears if we were Hannah!

But Hannah did not give up. Her faith gave her hope that God could give her a son. At the yearly feast at Shiloh, she slipped away to the tabernacle and prayed there. This was probably not her first prayer but rather one fervent prayer in many. Hannah prayed that if the Lord would give her a son, she would dedicate him to God for His service. God answered that prayer in Samuel.

66

It is difficult to know how dear this child was to Hannah. After years of prayer and longing, here was this loving bundle in her arms at last! From his birth until he was weaned, a little clock was ticking. Hannah wanted to use every minute to the best advantage. "How can I best show love to my little one so that he can someday show love to others? How can I prepare his tender soul to serve God? How can I teach him God's Law so that he will obey it?"

Even at a tender age, Samuel was being prepared for the future monumental task before him—to serve as a bridge in Hebrew history between the troubled times of the judges and the triumphant, if ill-fated, reign of the kings. He served as a prophet, priest, and judge. Samuel was a giant in spiritual history but he stands in the shadow of his great mother's faith.

Hannah, like Job, realized that children are lent to us from God and can be given and taken away. "Sons are a heritage from the Lord, children a reward from him" (Psalms 127:3). Children are not so much God-given gifts for us to keep as they are trusts for us as stewards to prepare and keep wisely for a time. They will not be in our care forever, and the time they are entrusted to us is precious.

Let us learn from Hannah. Hannah prayed that her child would be set aside for the Lord's service before he was born. That is where it ought to begin with us—before birth. May we be able to say with Hannah, "I prayed for this child, and the LORD has granted me what I asked of him. So now I give him to the LORD. For his whole life he will be given over to the LORD" (1 Samuel 1:27-28).

ANALYZING THE SOIL

It helps the farmer to stand back and take a look at his soil. Imagine the farmer stooping, scooping up some dirt in his hand, and sifting it through his weathered fingers. Is it black loam or red clay? Is it fine dust or clumpy with clods? Is it rich and ready to produce fruit, or is it infertile from years of misuse and neglect?

Analyzing the color, texture and condition of the farmer's soil tells him what he needs to do to get the best yield from that soil. So it is with our "soil." Different ages and stages of our children require unique approaches to obtain optimal results. In this chapter and the next four, we will try to look at different ages to see how their need can best be met and how they may best be reached with God's Word. These ideas for certain ages are not carved in stone but are general guidelines to use with our children.

WHAT MAKES A TOT TICK?

Enter baby—creative bundle of seemingly never-ending energy, disrupting households forever and causing even the grouchiest old man to smile! We wonder what we would do without our baby.

At first a baby learns by observation. An infant's eyes are his primary gateway to understanding everything around him. Research is showing that even newborns are capable of focusing their eyes. The baby is constantly visually processing all the sights around him. Vision helps him orient himself to the outside world. Before he can move by himself, grasp an object or even smile, he watches others and learns by observing. You realize this when he starts imitating the bad habits of his older siblings! Watch a baby's eyes sometime and you will see how he observes.

As he gets older, a baby learns by participation. You can attest to this when you think back to the times you tried to talk on the phone near a toddler. He is quick to want a piece of the action himself—chewing on the phone cord, wanting to climb on your lap, and pushing the number buttons. Or there is the worst offender—the secret marauder who takes advantage of your occupied state by pulling down the plant or heading for the bathroom to play in the toilet. This definitely is a participating age—in the good and bad sense!

Later a baby will learn by repetition. Why else does he keep throwing his cup off the high chair for you to retrieve for the 49th time? Experts say it teaches the baby "cause and effect." I think it teaches parents "patience"! When baby repeats an action over and over, the learning is imprinted in their minds.[1]

Let us keep these ideas in mind when we think about how tots learn, and especially how we can effectively teach and train them spiritually.

WHAT TOTS NEED

From birth to about the age of two, a child learns through a feeling-action response to the outside world. The Swiss psychologist Jean Piaget called this age the "Sensorimotor Stage." The child's reflexes react to needs and stimuli through his five senses—hearing, seeing, feeling, smelling and tasting. That is why he puts everything from his teething ring to your priceless heirloom bracelet into his mouth!

Just as babies must drink milk first to survive, so our babies must start on spiritual milk. Simple, brief stories would be best for these tots with their limited vocabulary and short attention span. A child at this age remembers from what he does—handwork, activities, games, songs he acts out. He needs colorful, touchable stimuli. The tot needs love, not fear, stressed in stories. He is very literal in his understanding so he does not understand analogies, symbols, or abstract ideas, such as object lessons. It would be hard for him to understand the idea of an all-powerful God who is everywhere. But he can begin to understand that Jesus is God's Son because he is a son of Mommy and Daddy.

During this period his parents, especially his father, stand in the place of God to him. Trust and love are developed and nurtured in the child through guidance and patient care from parents. Self-control and obedience in later years begin in behavior patterns set in these early years. What responsibility that places on the parents' shoulders!

Much research has been done on bonding, that initial interaction of caretaker with the infant. Bonding has sometimes been viewed as the emotional glue that binds babe and parents together forever. Some feel this early bonding has the capabilities of "Crazy Glue"—when you are stuck, you are stuck forever! But for that bond to last, parent and child must spend time together throughout life. Often parents spend weeks in childbirth training so that both parents may be present and experience the first precious moments together with the baby. But after the novelty of birth wears off and the tedious routines begin, it is back to work, back to recreation, back to "normal," with little time spent with the child.

This is especially true for the father. In most cases he spends much of his week at work away from the family. This is his God-given responsibility. It is estimated that the average father spends 50 hours a week sleeping, 40 hours working, and seven hours getting ready. What time does he spend with his children? Two and a half MINUTES a DAY![2] God has put special responsibility upon fathers to bear the role of spiritual leader in the Christian family. Note that fathers, not mothers, are commanded to bring up their children in the training and instruction of the Lord (Ephesians 6:4). Both parents are responsible, but it is the father's duty to be the spiritual leader. The child's overall view of God is influenced a great deal on how he sees his father.

"Train a child in the way he should go, and when he is old he will not turn from it" (Proverbs 22:6). It is interesting to note that the Hebrew word for "train" was a term used in regard to infants. During Solomon's reign, a midwife would take juice from dates and massage the gums and palate of the newborn. This action created a sensation of sucking and taste and the child would be more eager to feed from its mother's breast. The term came to mean "developing a thirst."

The term later came to be used in the training of a horse, as in "breaking and bringing into submission of a wild horse by a rope in the mouth."

Thus "developing a thirst" and "bringing into submission" evolved to mean "dedicate" and "consecrate." "Train" involves all of these. That means that parents should start bringing childen into submission and developing their taste for good things as early as possible.[3]

THE PLASTIC YEARS

They pass so quickly, the days of youth,
And the children change so fast,
And soon they harden in the mold,
And the plastic years are past.
Then shape their lives while they are young,
This be our prayer, our aim,
That every child we meet shall bear
The imprint of HIS name.

Author unknown

69

PREPARATION OF THE GARDENER

It is said that the early American Indian observed a solemn ceremony before he started building a new home. He would consecrate the ground on which his dwelling would stand. Such rituals mean little to us today, but the principle on which it is based is still significant.

Though the "home ground" might not be considered sacred, the home atmosphere plays an important role in the growth and happiness of its inhabitants. A peaceful, loving atmosphere where God reigns prepares its inhabitants to face with confidence a corrupt world. A troubled home atmosphere without God offers nothing better than the world outside its walls. A tense, unhappy environment can even affect the unborn child. Parents are the thermostats of their home climate; they determine whether it will be warm and supportive or cold and aloof.

How are we as parents setting the tone for spiritual growth? Do we have meaningful prayers in our homes? Is studying the Bible a delight or a drudgery? Has our quiet time with the Lord become a priority?

Do we smoke, even in secret? How about social drinking (just a little)? Do we gamble on the sly in the state lottery? Is swearing a problem? What are our excessive habits—eating, gossiping, criticizing? Why not get rid of them before our children arrive on the scene? What better incentive to get our lives and our home in shape!

It is difficult to pass on a faith which we do not possess ourselves. Let us prepare the home ground even before our little ones enter the world so we can pass on our faith to them. The influence of a prayerful, loving home from the very beginning of an infant's life cannot be overestimated.

BUILDING BLOCKS FOR THE TOT

One of the proudest and happiest times new parents can ever know is the day they take their little one home from the hospital. I remember it distinctly in my life. I felt like a queen on her throne, (even though it was mobile—a wheelchair!). My royal cushions were there (pillows to make sitting more comfortable!). I wanted it proclaimed from the rooftops, "Look at this beautiful child! Look what God has given us!" Nothing could mar the glory of that moment.

But glory is fleeting and reality sets in. The child is still beautiful and he or she is still ours. But sometime between the messy diapers and 3 A.M. feedings, we would question the child's beauty and ownership! How can I reach the bubbling, babbling creature with God's Word? Or can I reach him, period?

This age is one of preparation—the beginning of things to come. No, the one year old will not understand John 3:16 but he can learn that "Mom and Dad love me." Then Jesus' love for him will make more sense. Later on he can learn that Jesus loves not only him but the whole world. And much later, he will learn of the responsibility he has to take that simple message to the world. So knowledge is a building process and we start building soon after birth.

What are some of these building blocks that will give our tiny tot a good foundation?

1. GIVE HIM HIS OWN BIBLE. This Bible is not for reading but for holding and taking to church services. In reality, it will land in the child's mouth because everything else except the kitchen sink does! One person joked that they have never seen the Bible's admonition to "feed on me" taken so literally. Unfortunately, after the chewing stage, some of us never get our teeth into the Bible again!

The youngster needs to know early on that the Bible is a special book that tells about God and Jesus. He needs to learn to respect it and take care of it. I remember the words of a little song we taught the babies in nursery class:

> This is the Bible, We love the Bible.
> It is God's Word.
> We will be careful when we turn the pages,
> It is God's Word.

Then we let the babies turn the pages of the Bibles in front of them.

You might want to purchase a Bible that is sturdy enough for a toddler's use but will not be so expensive that some transparent tape to repair a torn page will upset you. A paperback version with pictures would do nicely later. We have been fortunate enough to obtain free, small Gideon New Testaments. They have been used in more ways than one, as the teeth marks attest!

MY FIRST BIBLE

> A little boy's first Bible is the greatest thrill he's known;
> There's a sweet, unique excitement in a Bible all his own!
> And yet my heart is smitten as this touching sight I see—
> Has his reverence for that Bible depended much on me?
> As I see him with his Bible, I bow my head and pray—
> May he always love that Bible the way he does today.
> Then I hear a voice within me speak in solemn words and true;
> How he cherishes that Bible will depend a lot on you!
> I love my Bible better since I've seen the beaming joy
> This wonderful possession has afforded to my boy.
> May I seek to give mine daily a devotion he can see,
> For the love he bears his Bible will depend a lot on me.
>
> Author Unknown

2. PRAY WITH HIM. How did Jesus answer his disciples' request, "Teach us to pray"? By praying with them. And that is how to teach our little ones to pray. Marian M. Schoolland wrote, "Prayer is the precious means of sealing to the child's

heart the seed that has just been sown."[4]

Your child might be too young to say a prayer but he is not too young to be affected by your prayers. At first you might bow by the crib at bedtime and say a few simple sentences to the Heavenly Father. As time goes on your child will come to expect this quiet time of communion even though he does not understand it. Later he will attempt a few sounds and then a few sounds in imitation of yours. Some children might find it easier to begin with hearing and then saying memorized prayers. Familiarity with printed prayers might help a young child find the words for his spontaneous prayer.

Thanking God at mealtime is another time to teach our children to pray. At this time the child can imitate the actions and observe the customs of the family. The child can learn to fold his hands and bow his head or cover his eyes with his hands to avoid distractions. Silent prayer would have little meaning to a child this age.

We can use opportunities to pray all through the day by keeping our prayers simple and within the child's experience, like friends, pets, and trips. Strive for more than "bless" or "gimme" prayers. It seems easier for a child to stick with the same opening such as "Dear God" or "Dear Father." Using different names for Jesus and God is confusing to a young child.

After a child can talk he can begin to use small phrases to pray. This is the beginning of our eventual goal—for the child to talk to God in his own words. He may repeat your words or may pray, expressing his own thoughts after you. He will want to pray, if we set a consistent example for him. Prayer can become meaningful to our little child only if it is meaningful to us.

3. SING SONGS TO HIM. Even as we feed, diaper, bathe and cuddle our infant we can sing. It does not have to be just baby songs or even children's songs. Why not expose the grand old hymns to our little one? Children learn to appreciate and love music that they have heard most often. This singing will be a blessing to you as well as him.

Research has shown that music and speech are stored in different parts of the brain. So when you sing a Bible thought or Bible verse to your young child, you are expanding your child's early learning even wider.

4. READ TO HIM. Jim Trelease, author of the excellent guide THE READ ALOUD HANDBOOK, advises parents to read to their child as soon as possible after birth. Why start so young? Understanding is not the purpose, at least at first. Rather, reading can have a conditioning, calming effect on the child. The soothing tone of voice combined with the security of a parent's lap is associated with attention, warmth and pretty pictures. It might even help a wiggle worm to settle down (at least for a few minutes!). Can you see the beneficial effects this could have on listening to Bible stories and remaining quiet in worship?

Besides boosting a child's imagination and listening skills, reading aloud has been shown to improve a child's grades and reading ability. In 1765 John Adams wrote that "a native American who cannot read or write is as rare an appearance as. . .a comet or an earthquake."[5] The reason for such verbal competence? From infancy the colonial child was exposed to daily oral reading of the Bible!

A good time for storytime would be any regular time when the child is tired enough to stay still—lunchtime, naptime, bedtime. It is best to allow some "settling down time" for everyone to review or to get in the mood of the story. A "Pay attention! Sit up straight! Settle down and be quiet!" does not make for receptive audiences!

With very young children a few minutes of reading aloud might be plenty. The time can be lengthened when the child is ready. Remember that this conditioning is gradual and applies to almost all ages and grades.

5. ATTEND CHURCH SERVICES REGULARLY. It seems ear infections, runny noses, and fifty other maladies affect the tot at this age. It would be easier just to say, "We'll stay at home from church until the child is two! If I take my healthy child to the nursery with all those OTHER runny nosed kids, mine will get sick. If I keep him with me during services, I feel like I've wrestled with a bear for two hours!" Then there is the problem of entertainment. To solve that, parents load up with something akin to a suitcase, filled with dry cereal, juice, toys, and other goodies.

It is an understatement to say that life with baby in worship services is no picnic! How does a parent cope? Some parents find a Worship Bag helpful.[6] It can teach the child to entertain himself while sitting quietly and still in worship. Hopefully in later years he will eventually listen to the sermon.

Even an infant can learn what is expected of him. The contents of the Worship Bag should be changed weekly to avoid boredom. Some items for the bag might be cloth books (some "quiet books" that teach learning skills such as buttoning and lacing), a small unbreakable mirror, soft blocks, and teething toys.

Please think twice about loading up your bag with a "mini-picnic" for your tot. There might be children who cannot make it through services without a snack. If your child must eat, please let him do it as discreetly as possible. It is difficult enough to deal with your own wiggly one without a picnic being spread before you two rows ahead! ("I want a cheerio, too, MAMA!") If you start bringing food, the child will expect it. If all else fails, perhaps a mint will hold him over until the service ends.

About this time or later, our children reach one of those grown-up thresholds. They discard those bulky diapers and make frequent, if not constant, visits to the toilet. But this stage is temporary—this too shall pass. It takes a parent's keen mind to differentiate between a child's real emergency and a desire to follow Freddy who left two minutes before. Please try to take care of the necessities of life like the toilet and drinks of water before, between and after services. It is so much less distracting to others.

LITTLE BY LITTLE

Starting these acts of worship—reading, singing and praying—is not only a conditioning exercise for our young tot. It conditions US to begin little by little—preparing the soil of our little ones' hearts. This age group has such a short attention span, we have to start small! But these little bits add up to make something much more important. Just think of the time we spend brushing our teeth—a few minutes of regular care can prevent ugly hole-filled pearlies, unhealthy gums and eventual loss of our chompers! Even one hour a week could not do what that few minutes does after every meal. So it is the regular bits of time and teaching that count.

In her book SEASONS OF THE HEART, Judy Miller compares these little bits to the pieces in a patchwork quilt.

> ...As I take each square or diamond shaped piece of fabric and blend each into the other for a delightful pattern, I think of the process by which I am weaving into the fabric of the children's lives the precepts of God's Word...
>
> So little by little, we take a scrap of truth here, a remnant of the gospel there, and we impart it into the lives of our children. When the pieces are joined together, a strong layer of values has been formed for children to build upon the rest of their lives.
>
> As we stand back and look at the finished product, a quilt or pillow top or whatever, we are overjoyed by the beauty and glad of the work that has gone into it. Just so, we may stand and look at our children's lives one day, and thank God for the finished product.[7]

This "little by little" principle is illustrated in the book of Isaiah,

> Whom shall he teach knowledge? and whom shall he make to understand doctrine? them that are weaned from the milk, and drawn from the breasts. For precept must be upon precept, line upon line, here a little, and there a little (Isaiah 28:9,10).

It would be wonderful if our children could say, "As long as I can remember I have sung, prayed and heard God's Word. I can't remember when I didn't go to Bible School. These things are ingrained in my soul and they show my parents' true love for me and for God."

Go get the Seed—it is time to start planting!

CHAPTER 8
PREPARING THE SOIL
Digging Deeper

1. What is meant by the statement that "the child should love God twenty years before he is born"?

2. Why was having a child so important to Hannah?

3. How are children like trusts rather than gifts?

4. How can the way a baby learns be described as "BABY SEE, BABY DO, BABY REPEAT"?

5. Why is the father so important in the whole, but especially the spiritual, development of the child?

6. Explain the Hebrew meaning of "train" in Proverbs 22:6. Why is it appropriate to use regarding infants as well as teenagers?

7. Why is it better to prepare the "home ground" before children arrive on the scene?

8. How does reading aloud to tots prepare them for Bible classes? Why is it better to have a regular story period with settling-in time?

9. How can we keep the young child's prayers from becoming just "gimme" and "bless" prayers?

10. What are some ways to expose babies to various kinds of spiritual songs?

CHAPTER NINE

Planting the Seed

"Once truth is firmly planted in a child, it continues steadfast through any test, but the planting has to be done early in the growing season."

Philip W. Bemis

"A good day for plantin,"' the farmer thinks as he reaches for his hoe and packets of seeds and heads for the garden. There in the dirt he drops the various seeds— tiny round ones, oval shaped ones, spindly tapered ones. Carefully he estimates the correct depth and distance between each row. He pats the soft earth gently over the seeds, as if tucking in a snuggly child at bedtime.

Planting seems to be such a simple task. If that was all there was to gardening, it would be so easy. But planting is just one stage in a continuing process of growth.

Our precious soil—our children's hearts—can be implanted with God's Word at any age. The oldest heart can be touched with God's loving message but it is frequently calloused by age and tradition. The younger heart is often more receptive.

TO TEACH THE YOUNG

It takes the kindest touch
To teach the very young;
To tend with loving care
The new growth just begun.

For only loving eyes
Can see the bud unfold;
Then humbly wait the blossom
And the beauty it must hold.

It takes the listening ear
To hear what children say

To answer what they ask of us
And show them wisdom's way.

It takes the calmest thought
To quiet restless youth;
The peaceful mind can point the way
To goodness, hope, and truth.

To teach the very young
With willing mind and heart
Opens wide the universe
Its treasures to impart.

Author unknown

The bubbly preschooler, aged two to five, can learn just about anything presented in an interesting way at his level. Just ask a typical four year old to sing a popular toy commercial from TV! How much more should these "livewires" be well-grounded in God's Truth!

Let us look at a biblical example of parents who implanted God's Word early and well in their child's heart.

AMRAM AND JOCHEBED

Of all those faithful listed in the Hebrews 11 "Hall of Faith," only one set of parents is mentioned. These parents were surely not the only faithful parents in the Hebrew nation, but their faith must have been noteworthy. In Hebrews 11:23 we read, "By faith Moses' parents hid him for three months after he was born, because they saw he was no ordinary child, and they were not afraid of the king's edict."

In spite of Pharaoh's command to throw all male newborns into the Nile River, Amram and Jochebed saw a purpose for Moses' life and refused to comply with the cruel order. We can see the care and planning that Moses' parents put into preserving his life. It took a brave and creative family to hide a crying baby for three months. Then Jochebed made an ark of bulrushes, waterproofed it and hid it in the reeds along the river. She had her daughter Miriam to stand watch over the floating cargo. Perhaps she placed the basket where Pharaoh's daughter often came to wash. Through God's providence Pharaoh's daughter decided to save the baby and obtained Moses' own mother for a nurse. Jochebed nursed Moses for a time until he was brought unto Pharaoh's daughter and "educated in all the wisdom of the Egyptians" (Acts 7:22). But he also must have been educated by his parents in God's ways. How else would he have known HIS people and been sympathetic to their cause enough to kill an Egyptian who was mistreating an Israelite?

The training given to Moses by his parents at an early age was such that all the years of education in Pharaoh's palace could not destroy it.

"By faith Moses, when he had grown up, refused to be known as the son of Pharaoh's daughter. He chose to be mistreated along with the people of God rather than to enjoy the pleasures of sin for a short time. He regarded disgrace for the sake of Christ as of greater value than the treasures of Egypt, because he was looking ahead to his reward. By faith he left Egypt; not fearing the king's anger; he persevered because he saw him who is invisible" (Hebrews 11:24-27).

Amram, Jochebed and their son tower as shining examples of faith to us in training and teaching our children. Their persistence and courage in the face of persecution makes our excuses seem quite lame! Our child might not be destined to become a Moses but God has a purpose for him in his kingdom. Let us prepare by planting the Seed early on tender soil.

ANALYZING THE SOIL

The typical preschooler plays, sleeps, eats, asks 30 questions per hour and has 579 wiggles per square inch! He is concerned primarily with himself rather than others. Sharing is not easy and should be encouraged rather than forced. He is beginning to understand and follow rules. The development of a conscience begins with the realization that there is "good" and "bad." He begins to identify with adults—especially his parents. It is easy to see the importance of providing a good Christian example to him.[1]

The child this age is unable to reason things out. His thinking is dichotomous; everything is black or white. Abstract concepts are beyond him but he is capable of understanding concrete ideas. He is curious, creative and willing to please. He learns by using his five senses and especially by doing. It is said that a child can remember only 12% of what he hears, 50% of what he sees, but 90% of what he does. Like the old Chinese Proverb: "I hear. . .and I forget. I see. . .and I remember. I do. . .and I understand."

Amazingly by the time they are three, these "little sponges" will have absorbed about 80 percent of the basic information they will need to cope in life! The rest of their life will be spent refining this existing knowledge base.[2] About 85 percent of an adult's personality is set by his sixth birthday! The first six years are so crucial. It is not impossible to change personality after that time, but it is increasingly more difficult as the years go by.[3] The Catholics have known this for a long time. In the sixteenth century Saint Francis Xavier said that if he were given children until they were seven, anyone could have them afterwards.

Experts tell us that each child has a style of learning, a way in which he learns best. Some children learn best by hearing (auditory), others by sight (visual) and still others through touch (kinesthetic). Why take a chance if you cannot figure out your child's learning style? Provide a variety of learning experiences with ample opportunity to touch, see and hear. How? An example would be instead of always teaching with felt tip markers, vary your approach with sandpaper, felt, pipe cleaners or yarn. Let the child tell the story again, using these tactile approaches. In this way he has heard, seen and touched and hopefully, this will make a more lasting impression.

The way a child is treated after misbehaving will influence his ideas of forgiveness and sin. If we wring confessions from him when he is just afraid of punishment or wants our forgiveness, what will he think of God? If we are patient but firm with our preschooler when he is untruthful, then he will see God more as a loving, merciful God than a stern, frightening tyrant. Through prayer and appropriate Bible stories he can better understand God's forgiveness, care, and love. How comforting that can be to a tender little heart![4]

The preschooler will have little concept of time until about the age of six or seven so he cannot understand sweeping spans of Bible history. But he can probably understand events in a person's life. Studies of Jesus, Joseph, Paul and others make suitable studies for this age.

TOO YOUNG FOR MEMORY WORK?

Are preschoolers too young for memory work? Some may balk that this age group is not mature enough to understand what they memorize and that memory efforts are wasted and possibly destructive. Others feel that though the child may not understand every word now, they will be stored away for later use. The key is making the memory verses as meaningful as possible to him now. After all, what is our goal in scripture memorization—to recite verses word-for-word or see little hearts touched and changed? Understanding, acceptance and application of Bible truths are what we truly seek.

Creating vivid visual images can greatly enhance memory, whether in learning memory verses, new songs, or Bible facts. A preschooler can more easily understand the concrete images of a cat, car or table than the abstract ideas of hate, envy or good. Dr. Jerry Lucas, a memory expert who has memorized the whole New Testament, recommends using pictures of objects or concepts to help the child visualize intangible ideas. Rebus pictures are excellent for this purpose.

How else can we make memory work easier for our children? Begin Bible stories with a picture, song or question. Dress up like one of the characters. Use eyes (eye contact), hands (gesturing) and voice (whispering and pausing). Bring in a Bible object of interest. Slow down and emphasize important points. Grab their attention![5]

With all the characteristics of a preschooler, it seems like a prime time for planting the Word of God in his heart! Let us look at some ideas to help with the sowing.

PLANTING THE SEED IN "BIBLE TIME"

Before too many outside activities pull the children in opposite directions, many families form the devotional habit. The preschool years offer a good time for establishing regular "Bible Times," also called devotionals, family devos or worship periods.

In one family the little boy shouted for everyone to come to the "commotion" and with little children that is not far from correct! To keep wiggling and distractions to a minimum, keep the Bible reading short to allow for a child's short attention span. Better to leave him eager and willing instead of worn out!

Make it easy to come together for this time. Have a regular time and a place set aside for the materials you need so you will not have to yell, "Has anyone seen the Bible story book?" Do not give a choice between T.V. or another favorite activity and Bible time. When you do not have much time, shorten the reading rather than skip it altogether.

Ideas for family devotionals are limited only by a parent's imagination. Some families with preschoolers follow the systematic study of Jesus' life in the gospels or the favorite stories in Genesis. Reading through a Bible story book gives continuity. Even more is accomplished when parents plan ahead and write down ideas in a devotional journal or notebook. By planning a week or two ahead, various ideas and materials can be utilized and collected beforehand, instead of running aroung gathering props while everyone else fidgets in the living room. This approach can also prevent the stagnation of always doing it the same old way.

One couple discovered Benjamin Franklin's list of thirteen virtues that he sought to develop. From this they went to the spiritual traits found in the Bible in 2 Peter 1:5-7; Philippians 4:7; and Matthew 5:3-12. They then arrived at their own list of character traits that they wanted their children to develop. With each of their thirteen traits, they emphasized the definition, a corresponding memory verse, and an appropriate new song to learn each week. They found stories of Bible characters, great people (historical and current) and other topics to amplify each character trait. This idea would work well with any theme.[6]

Above all, show enthusiasm yourself for Bible time! The eagerness we demonstrate will be reflected in our chilren. When you tell or read God's story, you can be one of the best visual aids by your gestures and voice. The Bible can be dramatic— let us make it that way!

METHODS OF PLANTING THE SEED

Various methods may be used to plant the seed in a child's heart. Here are some to consider.

READING ALOUD

1. BIBLE. When their son was four, one family read from a simplified version of Mark, chosen for its brevity. After the reading, the father played a game in which everyone must ask a question and answer one. Sometimes the questions moved to the left, other times to the right. This required careful listening because someone might "steal" the question a person had planned to ask and he would have to ask another one. At first the questios were simple—Who? What? Where? As time went on, other questions were introduced such as: Why? What does that mean? and later, What can we learn from that? Much was learned from such a simple approach.

2. BIBLE STORY BOOKS. The Bible story book can become a faithful, dogeared friend during the preschool years. The young child enjoys seeing the familiar book over and over. Be sure the Bible stories are colorfully illustrated and easy to understand. Some are even written to teach eager preschoolers to read.

One missionary mother in Argentina reads a brief picture story Bible book with questions after each story to her preschooler. When she first began he was quite restless but soon was able to answer most of the questions. She says now her 3-year old cannot go to sleep at night without his Bible story. Now that is the way to train both child and parent! It makes it easier for a child to know that bedtime is coming eventually (but what a pleasant way to end the day!).

3. LIBRARY BOOKS. Library books widen the choices of a home library with almost limitless possibilities. In her book HONEY FOR A CHILD'S HEART, Gladys Hunt provides an excellent bibliography which categorizes quality reading by age group. She states that childhood is too short to waste on mediocre books. Her list includes many good religious books as well as secular ones. Her religious suggestions should be checked for doctrinal problems before reading aloud. Picture books, adventure stories, biographies, poetry—she includes an interesting enough array to whet any child's reading appetite (parent's too!).

Let us look at an example of how a library picture book can further a child's interest and curiosity about ideas we sometimes take for granted.

In 1978 NOAH'S ARK won the Caldecott Medal, an award for the best illustrated children's book of a given year. Basically a picture book with few words, it would be perfect for discussion with your child. Peter Spier's ingenious illustrations invite even adults to think! His clever drawings might stimulate these questions: What was Noah's occupation before the flood? How much food and provisions would Noah have to stockpile for such a trip? What crude tools did Noah and his sons have to work with? Is it possible that many animals were caught and only the best were chosen? What about the sanitary conditions inside the ark? (Multiply the zookeeper's job a hundredfold!) Can you imagine what a mess the ark was after its inhabitants left? (Peter Spier's books, THE BOOK OF JONAH and PEOPLE, could be used just as imaginatively.)

None of these questions contradict what Scripture teaches and yet they help us understand and appreciate this story a little better. Sometimes I think we perceive Noah gently gathering the animals, willingly joining in line, two by two. There actually might have been some struggling, pulling, and pushing—especially in the case of donkeys! Hopefully this can give you some idea of how picture story books can enlarge on your teaching and make the story come alive.

Discussing pictures can also clear up misconceptions our children might have. In looking at NOAH'S ARK with my own son, I discovered a misunderstanding he had about the rainbow. We were talking about God's promise never to send a flood again and John said, "But that isn't true, Mom. There were the floods in West Virginia this year." I then explained God meant that he would never destroy the whole earth with a flood again.

MEMORIZING SCRIPTURE

Here are some ways which may make memorizing verses easier and more meaningful.

1. Learn the verse with your child.

2. Divide the verse into parts and repeat those parts until they are down pat; then put them all together.

3. Continue to repeat the verse until it is learned but stop before yawns of boredom.

4. Learn the reference, or as one preschooler called it, the "zip code."

5. Pantomime the verse when possible.

6. Draw a picture to go with the verse.

7. Put the verse to a familiar tune or make up your own music.

8. Put stars and stickers in a Bible verse booklet when the verse is mastered.

9. Show your child how he can apply the verse to his life.

Afterwards remind him of times when he succeeds.

SINGING

Singing is a natural way for preschoolers to learn. That is why so many commercials have simple but catchy tunes. Let us take a hint and put the Bible message into songs if we can. Several Christian songwriters have written Bible stories to familiar tunes and these are available at your Christian bookstore or through its catalog.

If a child is unsure of a song's meaning, she is more likely to put it into familiar words. So we can understand how one preschooler sang, "While shepherds washed their socks by night. . ." Then there was the total confusion in a family where the little boy wanted to sing the laundry song. His parents wondered which song that was so he belted out, "Bringing in the sheets!" His younger sister retorted, "No, no, it's bringing in the sheep!" A still younger sister replied, "You're both wrong—

it's bringing in the cheese!" And speaking of food, how about the young one's version of peace—"Peas, peas, wonderful peas."

I still remember my young rendition of "Low in the Grave He Lay." In Sunday morning worship my mind would envision my mother's noontime feast of delectable potato yeast rolls and chicken gravy as I sang, "Up from the gravy and rolls!"

Feel free to change the words of a song to make it easier to understand. Some parents taught "The B-I-B-L-E" to their young childen but felt hard pressed to explain the difficult metaphor "I stand alone on the Word of God" (except in the literal sense). So they changed that line to "I love to learn from the Word of God."[7] It is now much more meaningful to the children.

Songs for the preschooler should be simple and understandable; it is even better if they include movement. But that does not mean that every song we teach should be limited to clapping and stomping! While action songs might rivet his attention and keep his hands occupied, we can also introduce him to worshipful songs and hymns. We do not have to teach him every word perfectly. He will learn them by singing.

With a wealth of songs available, why not sing the best? Some songs are true to the Biblical record without losing appeal to children throughout several generations. Two simple ones come to mind. ONLY A LITTLE BOY DAVID gives several details, uses action to advantage and perhaps teaches a preschooler how many fingers he has, besides the "five little stones he took." Also ZACCHAEUS, a favorite of little ones, teaches correct details with appropriate actions. Contrast these with songs that teach little spiritual content. I do not hold these two songs up as the "spiritual standard" of preschool songs! I am just saying they teach something. Can we say that about all the songs our preschooler sings?

Now is when cooperation between parent and Bible school teacher is paramount. The parent can ask what songs are sung in class. The teacher can send home a list of songs that the class is learning. My son's four-year old class made songbooks with appropriate drawings. At home we taped those songs in the same order as the songbook. John taught me some new songs that day!

Songs that are learned during those preschool years usually last a lifetime. I am so grateful I learned the books of the New Testament in a song. I still sing it sometimes to find the position of the shorter books!

PRAYING

As prayer becomes a habit with the small child, there is a risk that it will become mere mechanical repetition. It may lack vitality and meaning, much like some adult prayers. One little girl had a solution to make her prayers more meaningful. She reasoned, "I always say the same thing to God every night so tonight I told him THE THREE BEARS for a change!" A college coed must have felt the same monotonous frustration. She said she wished her parents had never taught her

"Now I Lay Me Down To Sleep." The problem was not in that familiar prayer but rather that they had taught her nothing else.

How can we help our preschooler's prayers become more meaningful?

One way is to prepare ourselves and our child to pray. Picture the mother who suddenly glances at the clock, hurries the protesting kids to bed, and then commands them to bow their heads and pray. How meaningful will that prayer be? Contrast that to allowing the children to settle down a little and then asking questions like, "What will we talk to God about tonight?" Later perhaps they can be challenged further by "Let's include some things in our prayer that we have not said to God before." Taking time to think ahead encourages spontaneity from within the child much more than the order, "Pray!"

We can also begin to teach the real meaning of prayer. Jenny might think if she prays for a doll, it should appear on her doorstep the next day. By showing what prayer can and cannot do, we can help our children form right ideas about it.

Here are some ideas to vary our approach to prayer. Some may work; others may not. God just wants to hear from us—and often!

1. Read some prayers specifically for children.

2. Teach your child the Lord's prayer and pray it in unison.

3. Say a sentence prayer. Two people could rotate several times.

4. Either indoors or out, pray with open eyes, looking up at the stars and moon.

5. Pray for a new person each day. Lists will prevent repetition.

6. Make a picture book or poster on prayer. Divide it into sections: Things we ask God for; Things we thank God for; Things we say we are sorry for. Pictures can be drawn or cut from magazines to be glued in each section. The pictures would further conceptualize what the child is praying about.

DRAMATIZING STORIES

The "play's the thing" for a preschooler. Many preschoolers are real hams and they love acting on the "home stage." On the other hand, what better place to give the shy youngster encouragement than in the home setting. The home drama provides an outlet for both these types of personalities. Due to a limited "cast" (Dad, Mom and kids), everyone gets a good part and every child can be a "star!"

There are other advantages to a home production. Most Bible stories involve two or more scenes and the different rooms of the house do nicely for prisons, rooftops and temples. Families are brought together, especially when Dad plays a slave and Junior plays a king! Props are easy to find—bathrobes for Bible garments, yardsticks for staffs, pots for helmets and the list goes on.

Probably the children will want to do an encore. This extra practice will polish their "lines" and review the story at the same time. Do not worry about getting everything perfect. Just enjoy this with them and you will all learn. Usually everyone remembers a story better if he has acted it out.

Our family enjoys acting out Bible stories. A few days after we had premiered "Solomon's Wise Decision," our three and a half Amy said, "Let's get my baby and play Solomon!" She probably did not understand Solomon's great wisdom but the story had made an impression!

FINGER PLAYS

Finger plays are an excellent way to exercise wiggly hands and learn at the same time. I will include only one here because there are several finger play books available for a variety of Bible lessons. Remember this one? (Note the change to make it more accurate.)

"This is the church building.
This is the steeple.
Open the door
And here's the people." (or "Where's the people?")

VISUAL AIDS

Two preschool brothers were in different classes but had the same lessons for Vacation Bible School. When their mother asked them what the teacher talked about, one said, "It was neat, Mom. The Lord zapped Lot's wife and turned her into a pillow full of salt."

The other boy corrected, "You mean a pillar of salt. A pillar is like a tall pole. Our teacher drew us a picture."

The first son did not see anything to help him visualize what a pillar was so he imagined what he thought the teacher said. Visual aids are important in teaching our Bible stories because we are dealing with a different time, place and culture. Anything we can do to help a child see what we are talking about will make a more lasting impression.

"But I don't have any visual aids at home!" someone complains. Use what you have at home and investigate what resources might be available on loan. With the elders' or teachers' permission you might be able to borrow some equipment and visual aids.

Donnie and Mary Baker, in their excellent BIBLE STUDY GUIDE FOR ALL AGES, wrote that of all the visuals they used, homemade stick figure stories were the most effective. They found Bible story books often incomplete and inaccurate and flannelgraph pictures lacking in needed pictures. They believe that even the least artistic can teach a Bible story with stick men!

Taking this a step further, the Bakers helped each of their children compile a stick figure storybook about each major Bible character. These storybooks encouraged their children to tell and review the stories. They recommend saving these books for the family to enjoy in the future.

Here are some other visual aid ideas to vary your approach.

1. Flash Cards—Learn vocabulary words or put pictures from the story in correct sequence.

2. Posters—Draw pictures from the lesson as it is taught or use windows and doors to reveal parts of the lesson as you go.

3. Murals—Draw portions of a story or overview of a person's life or span of a cluster of events like the ten plagues. Even very young preschoolers can draw grass, dust, and stones.

4. Chalk Board—Draw stick men or emphasize words or Bible verses. Use colored chalk for extra "umph."

5. Puppets and Dolls—Use your child's ready-made ones or make some simple ones. Your homemade creations might include: finger puppets, spoon puppets, hand puppets, sock puppets and dolls made from paper, cork, spools, clothes pins, paper towel rolls, toilet paper rolls, detergent bottles or pipe cleaners.

6. Flip Books—Fasten pictures by rings or tape.

7. Styrofoam boards—Stick any figures in styrofoam for a 3-D effect. The boards can be painted various colors to represent earth, grass, or ocean.

8. Surprise Box—This box, covered with aluminum foil or wrapping paper, is really a means of spotlighting something to use in the lesson. The element of surprise makes it work.

9. Picture Wheels—A picture plate, with a triangular section cut away, can serve as a novel way to tell and later review the story.

Children will enjoy getting involved in these activities. They can tell the story again using your work or perhaps draw their own. When we ask them to tell us about their art, we can more easily see how they have grasped the story.

WHAT IS IN YOUR HAND? (OR YOUR CLOSET OR YOUR KITCHEN OR. . .)

Sometimes it is good to dust the cobwebs from our minds and think creatively like a preschooler. There are all kinds of teaching possibilities with simple everyday objects if we just look for them.

A lazy susan for salads turns into a "Bible story in the round" with scenes of Fisher-Price people or other figures. Packaged paper towels and toilet paper rolls become the walls of Jericho falling down. A watering can is transformed into clouds, emptying rain on Noah and the ark in a tub of water. Two blue moving scarves forms the Red Sea that parted for the Israelites. Crumpled aluminum foil is converted to Solomon's riches. Cotton from medicine bottles forms Abraham's beard.

With a little imagination, throw-away materials can be used in Bible art or craft projects for the preschooler. Here are some suggestions to use as a springboard for your own ideas.

1. Old newspapers—Paper-mache puppets
2. Cards in women's hose packages—Mini-posters for verses
3. Continuous computer printout paper—Murals for stories
4. Popsicle sticks—Sticks for paper puppets or crosses
5. Scraps of fabric—Textures for collages
6. Covered or painted boxes and cans—models of cities
7. Pieces of yarn and colored string—Stick pictures
8. Large paper grocery bags—Preschoolers' outfits

WORSHIPPING WITH THE PRESCHOOLER

The preschooler is learning to sit for longer periods of time but still has a short attention span. During church services, ward off his fits of fidgets with the Worship Bag. It can include stickers, sticker booklets, Bible coloring books, crayons, Bible puzzles and books that are changed weekly.

Do not bring out the bag until he needs diversion. To a limited extent the child this age can sing and bow in prayer with the congregation so encourage his participation. He can learn that during the Lord's Supper we remember Jesus. He will probably want to put money in the collection plate. Explain that the money we give does things for Jesus and is not given to him personally. Otherwise, literal-minded preschoolers might wonder if Jesus lives in the collection plate!

PLANTING GUIDE

As we try to plant God's Seed in our child's heart, perhaps the thoughts in this planting guide might inspire us!

Plant 4 rows of peas:
Preparedness
Perseverance
Prayer
Patience
Next plant 3 rows of squash:
Squash excuses
Squash criticism
Squash indifference
Then plant 5 rows of lettuce:
Let us teach in love
Let us train by example
Let us be diligent
Let us mirror the image of Christ
Let us be enthusiastic

No garden is complete without turnips
Turn up with a smile
Turn up with a new idea
Turn up with real determination.

CHAPTER 9
PLANTING THE SEED
Digging Deeper

1. What demonstrates that Amram and Jochebed instilled in Moses a love for God and His people?

2. What is meant by Saint Francis Xavier's statement, "Give me the children until they are seven and anyone may have them afterwards"?

3. What are some different styles of learning? Why is it best to utilize various learning experiences with our children?

3. Give specific examples of ways to make memory work easier for the preschooler.

4. How can having a regular place and time make our devotionals more effective for the preschooler? Why does it help to plan ahead?

5. How can picture books be used to stimulate questions and clarify misconceptions?

7. Why is it better for our preschoolers to sing songs that teach something?

8. What are some ways to teach our children the meaning of prayer?

9. Why are "home productions" an excellent way to make the Bible real to our children?

10. Why are visual aids so important in teaching the preschooler?

CHAPTER TEN

Nurturing the Soil

"The finest fertilizer on a gardener's ground are his own footprints." Ancient saying in agriculture

Under tolerable conditions the planted seed eventually produces a harvest. But with proper nourishment and water, along with regular cultivation and protection from disease, the harvest will be more bountiful. So the gardener puts forth the extra nurturing that brings forth plumper, juicier and more plentiful vegetables.

Nurture—the very word could be aptly used in any nursery whether speaking of baby plants or baby people! In Ephesians 6:4 the word is used regarding the training of children. "And, ye fathers, provoke not your children to wrath, but bring them up in the nurture and admonition of the Lord" (KJV). The gardener adds nutrients to the soil to get the highest yield. Likewise, we as parents must nurture our children with good nourishing things to obtain the greatest return of spiritual fruit. The extent of the harvest, on the most part, depends heavily on the amount of nurturing.

The elementary school years, otherwise known as the tweenage, provide a ripe time to nurture. The child can read, write and begin to think more abstractly. He is more independent in his work and play. The time between the eager, absorbent years of preschool and the tumultuous years of the teenage offer the parent an opportunity to drive home to the heart the Seed that was planted earlier.

Often parents take an avid interest in their preschooler's early academic learning but after kindergarten, they feel that their responsibility is over. By the same token, some Christian parents faithfully read their preschooler a nightly Bible story. However, when he starts to school and becomes involved in scouts, sports, and other activities, they feel they do not have the time. The child's enthusiasm for learning in both instances can die young if it is not nurtured.

Let us zero in on a young man who was properly nourished and nurtured in spiritual things.

FROM LOIS AND EUNICE TO TIMOTHY

A mother and grandma team have been immortalized throughout history—not for their award-winning quilts nor their apple dumplings—but for their consistent nurturing of their son and grandson with God's Word. Paul pays this maternal pair a lasting tribute when he wrote to Timothy.

I have been reminded of your sincere faith, which first lived in your grandmother Lois and in your mother Eunice and, I am persuaded, now lives in you also (2 Timothy 1:5).

But as for you, continue in what you have learned and have become convinced of, because you know those from whom you learned it, and how from infancy you have known the holy Scriptures, which are able to make you wise for salvation through faith in Christ Jesus (2 Timothy 3:14-15).

In these passages we see Scripture as the connecting link between the faith of the parent (and grandparent) and faith of the child. A child's faith is the fruit of his parents' labor of faith through the Word.

How great it must have been to live in such a godly household where God's Word was taught and lived by mother and grandmother. This teaching probably came only from the maternal side of the family. Timothy's father was a Greek and his influence is seen in the fact that Timothy was not circumcised, though his mother Eunice was a Jew (Acts 16:1-3). It is possible that his father was dead and his mother worked to support him and his grandmother. At any rate, we can see that Eunice and Lois diligently taught Timothy whether his father was dead spiritually or physically. They did not excuse their responsibility because of their added role and duty. They accepted their charge and were commended for it.

Could we be commended like Lois and Eunice? How well are we accepting our charge to nurture our children?

ANALYZING THE SOIL

The elementary school years are an opportune time for teaching God's Word to our children. Preschoolers charm us but their knowledge and experience is limited. The tweenager can grasp more Bible facts and applications. Sometimes teens challenge us with indifference or resistance but the tween is still eager to learn if he can be involved in an active way.

Children from ages six to twelve are expanding their relationships. School is a place not only for "book learning" but "people learning." Children must learn to cooperate and express their feelings to others. In conflict, they must learn to adapt or face the consequences. Learning about relationships in the Bible will help our tween better relate to those in his classroom.

Tweens are like wolves—they run in packs! They form secret clubs and like to be "one of the gang." They may have best friends and "bestest" friends but they still like playing in a group. This group urge can be utilized with the family members being brought together in devotional time. This togetherness gives children a feeling of security when the group plays such an important part in their lives.

Even though you would not know from the chaotic state of his room, the elementary school child thrives on structure and regimentation. Regular family devotions come natural to him in this context. Regular does not mean dull. To sustain interest, the format should be varied but not the regularity.

Active participation is a key to reaching elementary school aged children. These bundles of boundless energy are "perpetual motion personified" so why not channel it for good? Not only can our devotions be briskly-paced and full of activities but we can apply their learning to real situations in helping others.

Hero worship is an important part of these years. Teachers, musical groups, older friends, actors—all can arouse undying devotion from the tween. Parents can indirectly influence their child's choices by praising ministers, Christian athletes and Bible heroes with whom their child can identify.

Children of this age need rules and responsibilities so they can better understand the justice and mercy of God. The tween is more conscious of right and wrong and the rules of his parents, teachers and the Bible. Fairness becomes important to him and "That's not fair!" might be often heard. Hopefully parents can show that God is always fair, even if they are not. Children need to know that parents will break rules just as they do, but God will forgive us all if we repent.

Most importantly, this is the age when moral values and guidelines are set. Tweens can begin to understand basic Bible doctrines like God, Satan, salvation, faith, and grace. Issues like honesty, obedience, friendship, and loyalty are being settled in their minds. These children need to see God's Word not as a rigid rulebook but as a helpful guide for living. We want them not only to know right from wrong but to be able to make their own choices and decisions within the guidelines of the Bible. It is a crucial time when many children decide to obey the gospel.

WAYS TO NURTURE

How can we nurture the soil to give the Seed the best environment in which to grow and flourish? It is evident that every technique might not work well at every age. The enthusiastic first grader with a toothless grin is vastly different from the tall, gangly sixth grader in jeans. Still these methods can be varied to fit the age and interest of the tween. These activities are grouped for convenience and might span several grades.

MEMORIZING SCRIPTURES AND FACTS

The elementary years are excellent years for memorizing. The junior years—the ages of 9, 10, and 11—are called the Golden Years of Memory. During those years memory work is especially easy for the child and he is more willing to do it than later.

How did the ancient Jewish parents teach their sons and daughters the many laws of God? They used mnemonic devices like plays on words and acrostics to help them remember. An excellent example of this is Psalm 119, which is really an acrostic poem. The verse in each stanza starts with a letter of the Hebrew alphabet. We would do well to use whatever memory aids that will help us and our children remember God's Word. Here are some simple ones that could be used to help us remember.

1. Was Jacob married to Rebekkah or Rachel? Notice that the couple JAcob and RAchel have "a" as their second letters.

2. Note the alphabetical order of these nations and their country of captivity. ISRAEL went into ASSYRIAN captivity. JUDAH went into BABYLONIAN captivity. (h I__J k; A__B c)

3. Jesus rose from dead after 3 days. The Bible records 3 people He raised from the dead. (Daughter of Jairus, son of widow of Nain, and Lazarus.)

4. Use your five fingers for remembering the five divisions each of the Old and New Testaments.

No matter how ridiculous a memory crutch may seem, use it if it helps! Look for relationships that may help you and your child to lock in Truth.

We often underestimate the capacity of the brain of the school age child. We can encourage him to learn longer passages along with lists like books of the Bible and the twelve sons of Jacob. In fact, experts feel that teaching in whole units, like a full chapter or selected portion, imprints on the long-term memory more indelibly. Various factors such as age, motivation, length and time available play a part in the result. But usually we only tap a tiny reserve in learning Bible memory work.

MEMORIZATION GAMES

Games make memorizing more fun. Here are a few ideas to spur you on!

1. ERASE A WORD. Write a verse on a chalkboard. Children can erase one word at a time as they repeat the verse.

2. JUMBLED VERSES. Jumble cut-out words of a verse and let your child put them in the correct order. (Hide them for more fun.)

3. KEY WORDS. Emphasize key words by standing or showing an appropriate symbol when the word is said. For example, each time "love" is mentioned in 1 Corinthians 13, a red heart could be held up.

4. PASS IT ON. Holding a small version of a game ball, preferably in season, begin a scripture. After a few words, pass it on to someone who can recite a few more words, and so on. My son and I found this give and take helped him learn the books of the Old Testament.

5. BIBLE TIC-TAC-TOE. If you can repeat a designated verse, put an X or O in a square. If you cannot repeat it, pass the verse on to another family member who can. The first person with three symbols vertically, horizontally, or diagonally on the diagram wins.

STORY REVIEW GAMES

Review, review, and more review! But who says review has to be boring?

1. PICK A POCKET. Find an apron with lots of pockets. In each pocket put an object representing a part of the story or stories to review. As the child picks out each object, ask how it was involved in the story.

2. ROUND ROBIN STORY. Begin the Bible story, then stop and let your child continue. Take turns around the circle of family members.

3. CATCH IT! Tell the story and purposely introduce an incorrect fact. Hopefully someone will "catch it" and correct the mistake. He then tells the story until he makes another mistake. The person catching it continues.

4. RHYMING WORDS. Begin with "I'm thinking of a Bible person, place, or thing that rhymes with TABLE." The answer is Abel. You can give different levels of clues, depending on the age level.

5. QUICKSILVER. Bring out the letters from your Scrabble game or make your own letters on cardboard. Turn all the letters over. The first player says, "I'm thinking of a Bible person (or place or thing) that starts with. . ." and then turns over the letter. The one who guesses first correctly keeps that letter and turns over the next letter. The one with the most letters wins.

6. TAKE TWO. Have two stacks of cards. One stack contains letters of the alphabet; the other stack has topics like CITY, RIVER, PERSON, LAKE, MOUNTAIN, etc. Let the first player turn over both stacks. For example, name a mountain starting with an "H—Mt. Horeb." Since both stacks must be shuffled, the possibilities are endless. This game can make good use of a concordance or Bible dictionary.

7. BIBLE ABC's. List as many Bible people, places, or things beginning with letters of the alphabet. You can make this more challenging by adding Old Testament and New Testament classifications or by setting a timer. Or you could shorten this game by writing Bible words in an acrostic of each person's name.

8. ALIKE/DIFFERENT. Pick a pair of people, places, or things and ask how the pair was alike or different. For example, take Jesus and His father Joseph. A younger child might say that both names start with "J." An older child might perceive that both were carpenters. This classification game grows with the child.

9. TOPICAL PUNCH. See who can "punch in" the most Bible items under certain topics. These topics could include: parables, miracles, lakes, rivers, towns, trees, mountains, plants, kinds of money, birds, flowers.

10. NAME THAT BOOK. Answer the questions. "What book is named for its writer? recipient? what it talks about? chief character? literary form?"

11. BIBLIO NUMERO. Ask questions about numbers in the Bible. For example, "how many: years did Methuselah live? days in Creation? sheep were left to find the lost one? pieces of silver by which Jesus was betrayed?" Some people might find it fun to do Bible Math by taking different numbers found in the Bible and adding, subtracting, multiplying and dividing these numbers for the result.

12. BIBLE CHARADES. Act out a Bible character's life. Be sure distinctive clues are given. Everyone could dress in appropriate garb for an extra clue (John the Baptist wearing a leather belt or Lydia selling purple).

13. SWORD DRILL. With Bibles up but closed, a parent calls out, "Draw swords." She reads a scripture reference twice and then challenges, "Charge!" The first one who finds the verse, stands, and reads the entire scripture, is the winner. He could be given a small reward like a piece of gum with the verse rewrapped around it. (Vary the drill by asking where a certain Bible story is found.) The important thing here is to FIND the verse and speed hopefully will come. Some children will be challenged by sword drills; others will be discouraged when their fingers do not work as fast as they wish. Take a cue from your child. It might work better to reward each child when he finds the verse.

14. RHYMING RIDDLES. Compose (or help others compose) riddles to guess. Here's an example:

> A Benjamite king of Israel,
> I towered strong and tall.
> I hid among the baggage.
> My parents called me _____ (Did you guess "Saul"?)

15. WHO SAID IT? State familiar quotations and guess who said them. Some examples are: "It is more blessed to give than to receive." (Jesus) or "I know that my Redeemer lives." (Job)

16. YOU ARE THERE. Report on some Bible event as an "on the scene eyewitness." This first-person exercise can help us experience the feelings of some Bible character.

17. TIME LINE GAME. String up a clothesline or strong string and clothespin up cards of main Bible happenings or characters. Which came first—Gideon or David? Moses or Solomon? The flood or the Exodus? Seeing relationships between events will help put together parts of a whole scheme of God's plan. Children can place their names over 19?? because they are a part of history too!

22. GEO-GRAPHICS. Draw general maps of Bible lands for childeren to fill in places, cities and bodies of water. You do not have to be Rembrandt to make outlines of these areas!

MOVIES AND VIDEOS

I look forward to Easter every year—not for my own chocolate bunny—but for the hope that the TV networks will show some of the grand old religious movies. It seems to be only at Easter and Christmas that they even think along these lines! I am looking forward to the umpteenth time to viewing BEN HUR, THE ROBE, and THE TEN COMMANDMENTS. Religious movies have value for putting Bible-time customs and surroundings in perspective for the tween and adults as well. Being involved in a story can help us empathize with the characters. Films bear the mark of the religious beliefs of the director and producer so it is important to discuss any errors that are shown. Bring out the Bible to check any questions.

BIBLE BOWLS

An idea that has ignited enthusiasm for Bible learning with older tweens and teens is the Bible bowl. While it is encouraged and initiated in the congregation, it often takes root in the home where Bible drills are encouraged. Students form teams and pore over questions from parents or youth ministers. After being quizzed in oral and written exams in the local congregation, they travel to other congregations for competition and fun. Besides learning more about the Bible, they meet other young people who are interested in God's Word. Hopefully this competition will spark the flames of incentive of learning the Bible without burning it out.

SINGING

A modern-day missionary was widowed when her husband was attacked by primitive Indians. In her sorrow, her mind drifted back to her childhood when her parents had gone through their hymnbook a song each day. This experience helped her teach her daughter songs by heart and sustained her in loneliness.

We could do that too! Our children can easily learn worthless ditties from TV commercials. How much more meaningful spiritual songs could be to them as they face the difficulties of life.

Besides providing spiritual strength, learning a variety of songs can help the child appreciate different types of songs. When I was in the elementary grades of Vacation Bible School, the minister would ask us what songs we wanted to sing. We would often select "Consider the Lillies" or "O Lord Our Lord" in the back section of GREAT SONGS OF THE CHURCH. I am convinced that one of the reasons we liked to sing those more difficult songs was that they were THERE in the songbook! I believe this makes a point for selecting hymnals that include a well-rounded array of "psalms, hymns and spiritual songs," of classical works as well as meaningful newer ones. A catchy rhythm, notes, and words do not always make the most spiritual song. After all, the Lord is more concerned about the spiritual rhythm and beat of our hearts than the rhythm and beat of our music!

Singing was a definite part of my family life. I was fortunate to ride to school with my mother who taught school where I also attended. On these trips we sang a lot. I especially remember Mom teaching me the older songs that meant a lot to her. I think of my Dad's booming bass voice when I sing other songs. Whenever I hear those songs, I not only think of their content but especially of my parents' faith. They both still love to go to congregational singings.

A singing family does not guarantee professional singing quality but it will certainly ensure a heritage of spiritual richness that could last a lifetime. Here are some other ideas to give our singing an extra dimension.

1. Make a "Songbook Trivia" from details of often-sung hymns like "What does it mean to 'raise my Ebenezer'?"

2. Present a slide show, illustrating one or several hymns. One of the more meaningful presentations I have seen was a slide show inspired by Psalm 148 in the hymn "Hallelujah, Praise Jehovah." As the congregation sang each phrase, corresponding slides were shown. A family could take this on as a thought-provoking and visually stimulating project for the congregation.

3. Make a book illustrating favorite songs. One family selected pictures and prepared information on the history of the song along with the life of the writer. Especially meaningful to Christians are hymns by our brethren Tillit S. Tedlie and L.O. Sanderson. By understanding the background of the songs we sing, we will develop a greater appreciation for them.

4. Learn songs that are Bible texts. Some examples are: "Rejoice in the Lord," "The Steadfast Love of the Lord," and "I Can Do All Things."

APPLYING THE NUTRIENTS

When the farmer applies natural or manmade fertilizer to the soil, he has given the seed a much better chance to flourish. If those nutrients remain in a fertilizer sack or compost pile, they do not do the soil much good.

So it is with the good things—the nutrients—of God's Word. If we do not apply them in working combination with the soil and seed, the spiritual harvest will not be as bountiful. The Bible can be planted in the heart but if its truths are not applied, growth will be stunted. "Do not merely listen to the word, and so deceive yourselves. Do what it says" (James 1:22). "Why do you call me, 'Lord, Lord,' and do not do what I say?" (Luke 6:46).

Paul, speaking of children, said "...bring them up in the nurture and admonition of the Lord" (Ephesians 6:4 KJV). Here we see that teaching (admonition) must go hand in hand with training (nurture) for maximum Christian growth. If the teaching is not applied, is it truly learned?

Lawrence Richards in his book CREATIVE BIBLE TEACHING lists the different levels of learning and their definitions as follows:

1. Rote—to repeat with understanding
2. Recognition—to be familiar enough to recognize
3. Restatement—to say it in his own words
4. Relation—to see how it effects him
5. Realization—to live it

Often in our teaching we get no further than rote learning and rarely reach the realization of "living it" level. Because of limited time, even the best Bible school classes can only do so much to teach our child to apply his learning. He might listen to the lesson and next discuss what it means to him. The discussion might end with a prayer that everyone applies this lesson to his life. After the "amen" is said, he goes home and often nothing is different. Everyone lives the same as before.

While Bible classes can plan activities to make Christianity real, parents can make those Bible lessons come alive for themselves and their children by "doing." Here are some specific suggestions—you can probably think of others.

1. SEND A CARD to someone regularly (perhaps once a week). These would not have to be expensive store-bought cards. The children could make and design their own. In fact, their creative efforts might be more appreciated by the recipient. For convenience, keep cards and stamps on hand.

2. WRITE A LETTER. Smaller children can dictate letters to their parents. Older ones can compose short letters to not only their friends and relatives but those who are sick and imprisoned. How about sending letters to local, state and national government officials (even the President of the United States) that they are being prayed for in this home. Also newlyweds, newcomers, new parents, orphans, shut-ins, servicemen, visitors to services, and college students appreciate notes of greeting and encouragement. What better way to introduce children to world mission work than by grading World Bible School lessons or writing to a foreign missionary. Include Bible verses (written out—often verses are not looked up if only the references are given). Much can be done with pen and paper!

3. EMPATHIZE WITH OTHERS. Empathy, politeness, manners, consideration of others—all of these carry out Jesus' meaning of "Do unto others." The act of washing His disciple's feet was a simple act of humility—and manners. Our children will be more warmly received when they show respect and courtesy. We can give them a head start in getting along with others by guiding them with some basic rules. Let them practice in the home setting until they have confidence in public.

4. MAKE A VISIT. Depending on the circumstances, children can make short visits to a sick or elderly friend with their parents. They can even bring something they have made to cheer him. A plate of home-baked cookies or handcrafted keepsake will cheer the recipient and its maker. A "flower arrangement" of lollipops might make a sick child's day. Older children might have the opportunity to visit

cellmates in a jail with their parents and leave a Bible and some tracts. A casserole could be prepared together and delivered to a bereaved family or new parents. Think of all the home visits that Jesus made!

5. REMEMBER THE HANDICAPPED. Although great strides have been taken to make things easier for the handicapped, attitudes still have a way to go. We can help our child to be more accepting of the physically and mentally handicapped by providing opportunities to be with them and help them. Be open for chances to take Braille Bibles to the blind or to learn signing to speak with the deaf. (What an excellent family project!)

6. ADOPT A FRIEND. A "friend" could be a foreign orphan or elderly person with no family close-by. A combination of the above ideas could be concentrated on one specific person. If the orphan is smaller than your child, you might bundle up some of your child's nice clothes that are too small. (Would you want YOUR child to wear stained, torn clothes with missing buttons?)

EARLY BLOOMERS OR LATE BLOOMERS?

Our primary goal for teaching our children is for them to obey Christ and reach heaven—with us! But while many parents would do everything to accomplish that goal, they sometimes unknowingly quench the very desire of their children to become Christians.

When their little one—an early bloomer—approaches them about obeying the gospel, they say, "You're too young—wait until you know more." If the interest is shown but turned off, it can dwindle. Later in life when the child still has not become a Christian, he may have lost that original spark. It is better for one to obey the gospel early and then later to be baptized again, than to be discouraged against it and never obey the gospel.

On the other hand, there is the late bloomer—the child who waits and hesitates to take the big step. Some children want to be sure of this important decision; others are afraid to go in front of the congregation. Whatever the reason, they may take longer to act. Parents can encourage this child but not force him. Otherwise he will wonder who made the decision—him or his parents.

How important it is for parents to know each child and his degree of knowledge of God's Word. Then parents can guide and encourage him but know that the decision is ultimately up to the child.

FAMILY DEVOS

Besides providing spiritual continuity, family devos can encourage cohesiveness at a time when children need to relate to a group. (Remember the gang stage!) If every night devos are not possible, perhaps 15 minutes three or four nights can be set aside. If a certain time and place is set aside for this Bible worship, it is more likely that it will become a regular practice. Whatever the circumstances, the important thing is to do it!

Take the telephone off the hook or delay calls until later. Ask neighborhood children to join you or wait until your devo is over. If your children see you delay other activities for this priority, they will see how important it is to you and it will hopefully become important to them.

BOREDOM CHASERS

Here are some ideas that others have used to spark enthusiasm for more imaginative devotions.

1. One father, who leaves for work later in the morning, reads Scripture while the family eats breakfast.

2. One family made a story box which contains Bible stories and Scriptures on slips of paper. Each day a child draws one out before devotions. Since he chose it, the child takes more interest in the story. Parents can preselect stories that are appropriate for their children's age level.

3. Another family utilizes their congregation's unused Bible school workbooks which cannot be sent back to the publisher. These provide activities that the whole family works through together.

4. Occasionally one family lets the kids take charge of devos. The parents are surprised at their insights!

5. Sometimes at bedtime one father discusses topics of particular interest and need to each child. He uses Scripture, a religious article, or timely book.

6. One mother motivates her children to read notes with Scriptures on the refrigerator. She hides messages in the middle of the texts to direct the reader to homebaked cookies or other treat.

DEVO ACTIVITIES

Who said devos have to consist of a story, songs and a prayer? Varying the activities can keep enthusiasm fresh and "doing" enhances memory.

1. Make books of all forms and shapes. Draw stick-figure stories of Bible characters. Carry out the theme of the story with shaped books. For example, "Jesus' Death" could be in the shape of a cross. Flipbooks could be made by drawing figures a little different on each page. When the pages are flipped quickly, the figures move. How about a scrapbook of pictures of animals from the Bible with verses and lessons drawn from them. The possibilities are endless!

2. "Cook up" a lesson to make it more meaningful. Taste some "bitter herbs" when studying Passover. Cook a pot of lentils for the lesson of Esau selling his birthright. Buy some pita bread in connection with the Last Supper and demonstrate how the disciples "broke the bread."

3. Act out a Bible story or analogy with plenty of action. Older children could write a play to perform. Use your imagination in gathering props. A football helmet

can serve as a soldier's helmet; a garbage can lid can become the shield. A stick is transformed into his spear or sword. Cardboard with string is his breastplate. Do you see how this could illustrate the Christian soldier or aid in portraying Cornelius or the Philippian jailer?

4. After a Bible story is told, illustrate a favorite part of it with crayons, paint, chalk or markers. Murals can be drawn on butcher paper and can include various textures like yarn, sandpaper, or wallpaper.

5. Take advantage of your children's avid interests. For instance, if they love to fish, take a look at first century fishing methods and boats and contrast with fishing today.

PRIVATE DEVOS

After children learn to read, they can read the Bible on their own. It helps them to have enough time set aside, either in the morning or evening. Parents cannot expect the child to make his own time—usually they will have to encourage him and plan that time for him. One couple presented their recent kindergarten graduate a new lamp and bedside table. They extended his bedtime by one-half hour with the stipulation that he read his Bible during that time.

It might be helpful to let a child choose a notebook to write down some of his spiritual thoughts. Summarizing a passage or writing down what it means to him might prevent Bible reading from being an empty exercise.

One mother and father REQUIRED their children to read their bible every day. Is that going too far? Is REQUIRING our children to brush their teeth every day going too far?

DON'T FORGET. . .

Our principal goal in nurturing our children is to never let them forget the Lord. The wise man admonished, "Remember your Creator in the days of your youth, before the days of trouble come and the years approach when you will say, 'I find no pleasure in them'" (Ecclesiastes 12:1).

CHAPTER 10
NURTURING THE SOIL
Digging Deeper

1. Who did Paul commend in 2 Timothy 1:5 and why?

2. Why is school a good place for "people learning" as well as "book learning?"

3. How can we help channel our child's hero worship in the right direction?

4. What are the Golden Years of Memory and why are they called that?

5. What religious movies have made Bible life and times more realistic to you?

6. Find the hymns and spiritual songs in your song book that were written by Tillit S. Tedlie and L.O. Sanderson. Research the background of some of them.

7. Why does rote Bible learning by itself not carry through in daily living?

8. How do you feel is the best way to deal with early bloomers and late bloomers?

9. What time and place would be most effective in your home devos? Can you think of some ideas to spark interest?

CHAPTER ELEVEN

Watering Just Right

"Let my teaching fall like rain and my words descend like dew, like showers on new grass, like abundant rain on tender plants."

(Deuteronomy 32:2)

The inexperienced gardener might look at drooping plants in his home garden and run for the watering can. But too little water is not always the problem. Actually feeling the soil would tell him more about what is wrong. Is the earth moist, wet or bone dry? Does the soil have too little water—or too much?

The right amount of watering is important whether our gardens are physical or spiritual. Especially during the teenage years is it important to guage our "watering" or teaching for the "soil" of their hearts. Too little emphasis on godly things can be disastrous—teens might become apathetic or beligerent toward the church. But too much can bring on overkill and deluge any spiritual spark of interest.

When I was a child, I "helped" water the family garden. Our garden was at the bottom of a long hill (at least it seemed long to me!). I remember jostling that heavy pail, filled with as much water as I could muster, all the way down that hill and dumping it ALL on the first tomato plant I saw. My horrified parents ran over and said, "Nancy, not ALL the water on one plant! Give some water to all the plants." I am sure that poor drowned tomato plant never knew what hit it!

Some parents drench their spiritual gardens the same way. When some children reach the teen age, their parents see a red light that flashes "NOW OR NEVER." They make sure that the congregation has a youth director. (That is noble in itself but having a youth director does not guarantee true teenage Christians.) These parents suddenly cram spiritual adages down their teens' throats. They make a last ditch effort to "Christianize" their children. It just does not work—at least, not for long.

On the other hand, other parents feel they have it made when their children reach the teen age. They view their teenagers with a shrug of the shoulders that says, "They're old enough—let them make up their own minds about God and the church." So these teens choose their own friends, activities and goals—and they are not Christian choices.

Some parents try to ride the fence. They want their children at church services— but when the prom comes, it is more important. Modesty is fine—except when your daughter is chosen Valentine Sweetheart. Christian camps are great—until the family gets a membership at the Country Club pool.

Teens must make choices—and so must their parents. These choices will affect eternity. If these choices are based on the Word, then both parents and children will have a groundwork, a foundation, a root system on which to function. That root system will carry them through the crises and challenges of life. In the topsy-turvy world of the teenager, roots must go deep and the watering must reach them.

It has been said the tallest tree sends its roots into the soil most deeply. For our spiritual garden to grow tall and strong, the roots must be deep and firm. That means our watering should be constant and gentle enough to penetrate the hardest soil to reach the roots below. The Seed of God planted in a fertile heart will put out the roots necessary for spiritual growth. They will support the plant against any storm and a fruitful harvest can be anticipated.

Let us look at one whose well-grounded roots in God's Word held him firm in spite of life's crises.

FROM PERSECUTOR TO PERSECUTED

Saul of Tarsus thought he had his life all figured out. This "Hebrew of Hebrews" had cause to be proud. His hometown was Tarsus, known as a bustling center of commerce. He was entitled to the privileges of a Roman born citizen. Most importantly, he was thoroughly trained in the Jewish law.

Of his own religious upbringing, Paul (his Roman name) said,

The Jews all know the way I have lived ever since I was a child, from the beginning of my life in my own country, and also in Jerusalem. They have known me for a long time and can testify, if they are willing, that according to the strictest sect of our religion, I lived as a Pharisee (Acts 26:4-5).

From the Bible we actually know little of Paul's home except that he had a sister (Acts 23:16) and that his father was a Pharisee (Acts 23:6). But he probably experienced the rigorous home spiritual training of a promising young Jewish boy of his day.

Usually a Hebrew child was taught moral and spiritual values by his mother until he was five. While girls continued to learn from their mother until marriage, boys learned a trade from their father as soon as they were old enough to help.

103

It is possible that Paul began to learn the trade of tentmaking at this time. The father then also served as the primary teacher, even though the mother shared this responsibility. It is easy to see how informal teaching could occur with father and son working side by side.

In New Testament times synagogue schools were established for male Jews to attend. At the age of about six or seven the boys would attend "the House of the Book," so-named because the lessonbook was the Book of the Law. Those first few years were spent reading the Scriptures.

The lad of ten years began studying the Law by oral repetition or *mishnah*. The teacher would read a sentence and the students would recite it together until they knew it from memory. This constant repetition engraved the Holy Writ on the learners' hearts. Paul's own lifelong familiarity is evidenced by his frequent quoting from the Law and the Prophets.

At thirteen a Jewish son became "a son of the Commandment." Childhood was over and he began preparing for his life's work. Public schooling was left for the practical education of learning a trade in earnest. Since rabbis received little or no pay for their work, this education was a necessity for the future rabbi Paul.

Around the age of fifteen, more serious students like Paul traveled to Jerusalem to study under a rabbi, such as the wise and revered Gamaliel. Gamaliel was known for his broadmindedness and courage of conviction (Acts 5:34). Paul was literally "educated at his feet" for the teacher sat on an elevated platform while the students sat around him on the floor. Here they dealt with the deeper investigation of the Scriptures.[1] Paul says of his training, "I was advancing in Judaism beyond many Jews of my own age and was extremely zealous for the traditions of my fathers" (Galatians 1:14).

With such a background, we can see how Paul thought he had it all together spiritually. In fact he was so zealous for his Jewish way of thinking that he was ready to persecute and kill any who challenged it. It was on one of these "seek and destroy" missions that Paul experienced the brilliance of the Son that transformed his life. He says of this change:

> Even though I was once a blasphemer and a persecutor and a violent man, I was shown mercy because I acted in ignorance and unbelief. . .Christ Jesus came into the world to save sinners—of whom I am the worst. But for that very reason I was shown mercy so that in me, the worst of sinners, Christ Jesus might display his unlimited patience as an example for those who would believe on him and receive eternal life (1 Timothy 1:13, 15b-16).

Paul's encounter with Christ brought him face to face, not only with the Lord, but with the job that the Lord wanted him to do. His true knowledge of God would not come through performing works of the Law but rather in obeying the will of Christ. His knowledge of the Law, beginning from childhood and continuing in later years, would be the basis which helped to tie the tempestuous loose ends of his life together. His earlier spiritual training prepared him for the debating, controversy and trials ahead. The use of Scripture in his sermons convinced many of his listeners of the truth and superiority of Christ's law. God's Word served as a link from the past to the present in Paul's understanding of where he fit into God's plan.

TEENS FACE CRISES

Like Paul of the past, teens today face personal identity dilemmas and moral choices. They wonder about questions like: Who am I really? What am I doing here? Why was I put here in this place and time? What is right or wrong? How can I best use my life? What occupation should I follow? Do my parents really care? Does God really care?

With soaring rates of teen suicide, drug use, abortion, and unwed parenthood, it seems that the answers to life's questions are being discovered in the wrong places. Choices are being made but there is no firm basis for the selection. God's Word must be the foundation for these decisions. Not only must teens be taught what to do but how and why to do it. They not only need instructions but exercise in decision-making based on the Bible. This teaching must begin before the teen crosses the threshold of his thirteenth birthday! Eventually the teen must make his own decisions without Mom and Dad to supervise. Perhaps their teaching will echo in his ears but it will depend on him to decide. How mature will his choices be?

ANALYZING THE SOIL

The heart or the soil of the teenager presents a special challenge because understanding the teen is no easy task. It is difficult to generalize about the characteristics of teenagers because they seem to change so quickly. The teen age is often like a roller coaster ride, full of ups and downs. It may be an exhilarating experience but when the ride comes to a halt, everyone usually sighs with relief!

Emotions and moods run the gamut in this age group. Feelings range from the highs of ecstacy to the lows of despair. It is a time for falling in and out of love. The teen's self-image is constantly on the line and at times, it does not fare too well.

There are variations in physical growth. Boys and girls of the same age may differ drastically in size and shape. Their rapidly growing, sometimes awkward, bodies make them feel unable to control factors in their lives and this uncertainty surfaces in other areas. It certainly does not help a teen's social confidence when pimples appear just before a big date or he trips over his feet![2]

The teen wants to be loyal to something or someone. Why else is his room plastered with posters of the latest singing star? Why else does he speak of "my friends," "our team," and "my school"? Girls have their "you'll-die-when-you-hear-this-secret" friends and boys have their buddies. For some, this is carried to extremes by excluding those not in "the group" or by even committing crimes to stay a part of the gang. This loyal spirit can be aimed in the right direction. We as parents must first be loyal to Christ and the church ourselves. Then we can teach the teen to be loyal to the Best Friend anyone ever had. His friendship will never let him down.

Along with this sense of belonging and loyalty is the need for approval. Peer pressure is one of the greatest forces a teenager can feel and he might go against his conscience just to get the crowd's approval. Not only should we instill the right set of values but also nurture the self-confidence whereby one makes courageous decisions. The "Just Say No" antidrug campaign could be applied to other temptations as well. We need to find positive sources for teen approval and get teens involved so they will feel needed and wanted.

In this fragile time in their lives, teens are looking for something to believe in. When teens are dealt with in a fair, kind spirit, they can respect those in charge. But sometimes their authority figures are inconsistent and unclear about their expectations. Do we wonder that teens turn to other things that seem to fill this void?

At times teens seem to retreat into their shells. Psychologists call this process "inwardizing." This time spent in their rooms musing, thinking, brooding is frustrating to parents but actually serves a purpose. The teen is trying to figure things out and sometimes he just needs time and privacy to think on his own. This is a time for the teen to probe the inequities of life and to ask questions about his faith. When this inwardizing becomes too long or frequent, the parent can try to pull his teen out of his mood. If we do not pry but keep the communication lines open, we will know better when to listen and when to answer questions.

Teens do not want to look "too good." It is a confusing time because to them it looks so "good" to look "bad." With the world flaunting sin in their faces, no wonder following the crowd in evil is so appealing. They want to be tough. It is our responsibility to show them it takes the tougher teen to say "no" to temptation.

Some teenagers ease through this transition into adulthood with few emotional ripples. Others barge head first, scattering people, usually their poor parents, along the way! Still others pass through slowly and awkwardly after hours of introspection and self-analysis. Each teen has his own way and rate of growth.[3]

START WHERE THEY ARE

As each teen must grow emotionally and physically in his own time, so must he mature at his own rate spiritually. Just as the seed in the soil grows at its own speed so the Word must take root in the heart in its own time. We can help the process but we cannot rush it—no more than a farmer can urge the plant to break through the soil before it is ready.

Not only must we let our teens take their own time to grow but in our teaching we should begin at their spiritual level, not at our own or anyone else's. If we start with "meat" when they are ready for "milk," they will not understand and be turned off to spiritual things.

Jesus, our Master Teacher, did not discuss complexities of the nature of the Godhead or theological aspects about miracles. He taught the people His profound message in a way they could comprehend—in simple parables.

In teaching the eunuch, Philip did not begin at the marvels of heaven nor at the miracle of creation. Rather he began "at the very passage of scripture"—where the eunuch was—and taught him about Jesus (Acts 8:35).

In Athens, the cultural center of learning and philosophy, Paul did not begin his sermon on Mars Hill about the merits of the Jewish religion or the attributes of the Christian faith. He began with their own gods—and went from there.

Christian parents must begin where their teens are spiritually. If they have not trained their children in their younger years, they cannot retrace their steps but they can start where they are at that point. One father became a Christian when his children were teenagers. Taking his responsibility seriously, he wanted to grow himself and also teach his children. He started to read to them from the Bible. Since they all did not know much about God's Word, they started with the basics. They began where they ALL were.

On the other hand, teenagers might react negatively to certain types of teaching. Some Christian parents had faithfully taught their children from infancy in a daily Bible story time. The mother used different methods so the children had no lack of variety. But when the daughter was in junior high, she objected to family devotionals, especially when her friends came to visit. It seemed that her friends thought that all the preacher's family ever did was sit around and study the Bible. The parents could have forced the issue but they did not. They realized that their children had been extensively trained and perhaps were ready for a different approach. Instead they explained that the important thing was to read and study whether with the family or alone. They encouraged private study time and provided opportunities for further spiritual growth. The children remain faithful Christians today.

It all goes back to knowing our children and taking them where they are. We cannot rush their growth but we can encourage gently, but persistently. Just like the gardener with the watering can. . .

SECRET DRAINS ON THE WATER SUPPLY

One year our family cultivated a large garden plot. We were excited at the prospects of fresh tomatoes, cucumbers, potatoes, green beans, corn and squash.

107

But there was something that loomed between us and a more fruitful harvest. A tall beautiful pine tree flourished alongside our garden. The shade from its lofty branches threatened to keep the sun from our developing plants.

But the shade was not the foremost danger. The far-reaching roots gulped up the precious underground water supply to quench their own immense thirst. Clearly, the hidden danger was worse than the visible one. The tree had to be cut down for our garden to be fruitful.

Sometimes things secretly sap the spiritual strength of our teens. On the sufrace they seem fine but under the quiet moodiness, a turbulent storm is brewing. The inward identity crisis and outward pressures from peers, changing moral values, high divorce rates, glorification of violence, and "the success at all costs syndrome" causes confusion. Many times this results in teenage pregnancies, anorexia nervosa, drug abuse, and the tragic ultimate end—suicide.

Psychiatrists who work with troubled young people tell us the answer that teens seek is finding a reason to live. That reason, found through God's Word, is in Christ and His church. It is the job of parents to help them find the reason to live—and live "more abundantly." If we listen, look and learn from our teens, we will notice subtle signs or more overt changes in behavior that might disclose these secret drains of their spiritual health. By prayer, study and God's help, we can communicate and bring their questions into the open for solutions. We can show them a reason to live.

WATERING CAN READY?

Why do watering cans have small holes instead of large half inch ones? A gentle steady shower of water is a great deal kinder to the developing plant than a rushing torrent. A deluge of water could break the stems and erode the valuable topsoil.

This does not mean that the gardener should not water well, however. If he soaks the soil for a considerable depth, the plants will be able to sink deep, healthy roots. When the hot sun dries up the surface moisture or when drought occurs, the roots can still draw on the deep "water bank" and keep on thriving. It is probably best to water deeply and less frequently.

Spiritually, perhaps it is best to water deeply and less frequently. Gone are the days when parents hold ultimate influence over their teens. Peers, movies, music, TV, fashion, school, sports, and clubs are vying for their time and attention. We must use those chunks of time we have to teach and train them to become the young Christian leaders they can be.

WATERING THROUGH THE CHURCH

Since peers are so important to teens, it is essential to provide activities to bring Christian teens together in study, fun and fellowship. This does not mean every activity has to be entertaining; yet it does not mean that it must be boring either.

How dare we take these vibrant young people and bore them to tears with meaningless classes and projects! Let us get them involved and let them know they are important. Here are some things the parent can do to encourage active participation through the church.

1. Some teens sit as a group toward the front during worship services. This discourages misbehavior and serves as a good example to the rest of the congregation.

2. Teens might find notetaking helps them concentrate on the sermon. Beware, however, if you have a budding artist or doodler. Perhaps he would be better empty-handed except for a Bible.

3. Some congregations have initiated TNT (TEACH 'N TRAIN) programs which concentrate on various Christian areas in which teens can serve.

4. Young women could be encouraged to teach or become teachers' aides.

5. Especially important is the training of young men to preach, teach, and read Scripture effectively. Every boy might not choose to preach fulltime, although we want to encourage capable young men to do just that! But whatever they might be for the Lord, they still are needed to take an active part in the public worship. We can give them practice at home and also in a training class. Then they should be given an opportunity as soon as they are willing.

6. Cooperate with the youth leader, if the congregation has one. Youth at this age like to feel they can confide in and look up to someone other than their parents.

FAMILY NIGHTS

Devotionals or Bible times will take a different twist during the teenage years. A parent cannot take a lumbering six-foot teenager on his knee for a cozy Bible story! And there might not be much daily time when the family is together. Be flexible and try to work something out. Use your ingenuity!

"Family Night" fits the bill for some families. Once a week TV is turned off and the phone is unplugged. Barring rare exceptions, social invitations are declined, church obligations reshuffled and personal activities postponed. All this trouble is taken to get the family together for learning from God's Word—and fun! Setting aside that evening with today's busy schedules is not easy but it is well worth it.

Mom and Dad cannot just sit down and automatically think up 52 super Family Night ideas! But asking their teens for ideas and keeping a folder of inspirations from bulletins, newspapers, magazines and sermons gives them a head start.

These weekly times are not meant to be somber ritualistic duties that are looked forward to with as much zest as a tooth extraction! Rather they should be kid-oriented and enjoyable. Who says Scripture must be boring and irrelevant to the teen's life? The Word is not boring but I am afraid we sometimes teach it that way.

Variety is what makes the difference. Change the location—sit on a blanket outside, meet in a bedroom or gather around a fireplace. Vary the teaching method.

Include different games and family activities to make this YOUR unique family time—a period when you not only grow close to God but to each other. We all need that but especially teens.

Instead of being preachy, we should have the attitude of "Let's find something Dad and Mom need to hear." The following topics based on God's Word might work well in discussions with teens: Sex, Dating, Marriage, AIDS, Finances, Personal Purity, Friendship, Work, Race Relationships, Church, Honesty, History of the Bible, Peer Pressure, Ethics, Entertainment, Fear, Will of God, Suicide, Death, Self-worth, Cheating, Teens of the Bible, Great Men and Women of Faith.

Here is a sampling of specific ideas for family discussions and projects.

1. One week make and wrap gifts. The next week deliver them to patients in a nursing home or children's hospital.

2. After reading from Proverbs for a week, write some proverbs in your own words.

3. Ask thought-provoking questions like: "What can I do to increase my faith? How can my prayers be more effective? What is my greatest spiritual strength? weakness? How can I increase my outreach for Christ to others in need?" Allow enough time for soul searching.

4. Since friendship is so important at this time, talk about the three braid cord of friendship in Ecclesiastes 4:12. These could represent ourselves, our friends and God. Some related verses are Proverbs 17:17; Proverbs 18:24; and John 15:13-15. The family could start working on a braided rug as a group project.

5. Begin questions with "Why do you think. . ." "What do you suppose. . ." "Can you remember. . ." Do not say a person's name at first or the others might stop thinking!

6. Since problem solving is a necessary step on the road to maturity, give your teens some practice. Open a "can of worms," a can with slips of paper with thorny, real-life problems with no easy solutions. Save clippings from newspapers and magazines that show how some people solved their problems. Brainstorm for possible solutions. Look to God's Word for helpful insights. This is especially useful when a family member has a specific problem.

7. Take advantage of a teen's interest in writing. Encourage him to write poems, dramas, tracts, diaries or journals of Bible characters, paraphrases of Scripture, reports about Biblical topics, and letters to missionaries and the elderly. Some of these might be shared in a brotherhood publication or congregtion's bulletin. As a congregational project, perhaps one issue of the bulletin could be devoted to the teens' creative efforts.

8. Is your dauther interested in beauty and fashion? Make a study of styles and beauty techniques of Bible times. Learn about the first recorded beauty show in Esther. Discuss modesty then (Bathsheba, Salome) and now.

9. Is your son interested in sports? Discover the Roman methods of training athletes. Look into the origins of the Greek Olympics. Compare these with the

references in the New Testament to the athlete in the Christian race—". . .I have finished the race. . ." (2 Timothy 3:7; 2 Timothy 2:5; etc.).

10. Study the qualities of the virtuous woman in Proverbs 31. While this is aimed at girls, boys would benefit from knowing what to look for in a wife!

11. Look at the attributes of the Christian soldier in Ephesians 6:10-18 and compare the armor with the Roman soldier's attire.

12. Explore the history of the church and how it relates to us today. Unfortunately all many teens know about Calvin is that he designs jeans! All they know about Campbell is that he makes soup! Knowing more about the early church, the Reformation, and the Restoration will give our children a taste of the great price men have paid to keep the Seed sown. Look for well-written biographies and histories to make these times and people come alive.

13. Examine "character complexes" and ask, "Do I sometimes have these complexes?" and "How can God help me deal with them?"

Jonah Complex—"If I get far enough away, God can't see what I do."
Elijah Complex—"I'm the only one left serving God while everyone else is evil."
Eve Complex—"One little bit of sin won't hurt."
Jacob Complex—"Lying is O.K. if I benefit."

(What other character complexes can you think of?)

14. To grab teen's attention use shock appeal. Hide a paper skeleton in your closet. Use it as a lead-in to a discussion on secret sins—the "skeletons in our closets." This is not to force us to "confess all" but to be aware that God sees all whether others see or not. Pray for forgiveness.

15. We can face problems of life in these three ways—by FIGHTING, FLEEING or FLOWING. Give examples of how Bible characters faced difficulties of their lives. Look at examples in your own life.

16. Discuss occupations of interest to your teen. How can each of these occupations be used for God's service? Remember Paul's "whatever you do in word or deed, do all in the name of the Lord." Find out about the opportunities of being occupational missionaries. Discuss how Paul used his skill of tentmaking to make his living, though his main purpose was preaching the Word.

17. Strike a chord of interest with your teenager if he likes music. Check out the music at your Christian bookstore. Encourage him to compose songs from his feelings or from Scriptures. Sing his compositions at your devos.

18. Can your teen draw or paint well? He could make a mobile of the fruit of the spirit (Galatians 5:22-23) or a "travel poster," commissioned by Caleb and Joshua to entice the Israelites to enter Canaan Land.

MAKING IT REAL

It is thrilling to see our teenagers demonstrate some of the fruit of Christian maturity. We can encourage that maturity by asking more and expecting more of them. Along with learning from the Word, the teenager can take an active role in the church, publicly and privately. This is an opportune time for discovering one's gift for service. Just look at what teens can do!

1. To practice hospitality, invite other teens and college students over for home-baked goodies. They could even have a baking party to send cookies to college students and armed service personnel away from home.

2. Babysit for parents who are visiting and holding Bible studies. What better experience to prepare teens for their own children one day!

3. Plan a "Mother's Day Out" program on Saturdays or one day a week during the summer. Teens could prepare hot meals (if lunch is included) and teach Bible classes.

4. Grade Bible correspondence courses. Look into the possibilities of World Bible School.

5. Choose a room in the hospital and visit there weekly. Offer to help the occupant however you can.

6. Wash the baptismal clothing after baptisms.

7. Prepare materials for and help with the bus program.

8. Collect and repair clothing for the poor.

9. Sew new clothes for orphans.

10. Conduct a religious survey of your town.

11. Grow flowers, arrange them and take them to shut-ins.

12. Keep a balanced food supply ready for the needy.

13. Decorate the pulpit area or the vestibule of the building.

14. Be a Christian camp counselor.

15. Plan a junior/senior banquet to honor graduates.

16. Prepare the Lord's Supper.

17. Help with the church bulletin and other office work.

18. Sew curtains for the church classrooms.

19. Keep bulletin boards up-to-date in the church building.

20. Prepare and participate in Bible Bowls.

21. Get involved with MADD (Mothers Against Drunk Driving).

22. Hold a visual aid work day to design visuals to send to missionaries.

23. Under the supervision of the elders, take an active part in planning youth activities.

SOAKING UP THE MOISTURE

We can water and water and water but if the soil does not absorb the moisture, what is the use? The proof of absorption is action. If the leaves wilt, we know that somehow the watering is not effective. But if the stems grow longer and the leaves look green and healthy, then we know the water is getting through.

The same is true of our teen's heart. Here again, proof of absorption is action. Are we choking them with overkill preaching or are we gently but firmly training? Are we letting them breathe? Or do we need to change our approach? Is our teaching making a difference in their lives?

CHAPTER 11
WATERING JUST RIGHT
Digging Deeper

1. Why is it necessary for teens to have a foundation on which to base their decision-making?

2. Who called himself a "Hebrew of Hebrews" and why did he have reason to be proud?

3. How did Jewish parents share the responsibility of training their young children? How did a girl's education differ from a boy's?

4. What was the "House of the Book" and who attended there?

5. Why did the synagogue teacher use *mishnah* in teaching his students?

6. Contrast the formal training of a promising Jewish young man, leaving home to study in Jerusalem, to the college student today.

7. How did Paul's early roots in learning the Law help him make wise decisions when he was older?

8. How does the teen's insecurity show itself in physical as well as spiritual and social ways? What purpose does a teen's "inwardizing" serve?

9. Why is it best to start teaching teens at the point where they are spiritually?

10. Why should topics like sex, dating, and marriage be dealt with in the home?

CHAPTER TWELVE

Pulling the Weeds

"Let us not become weary in doing good, for at the proper time we will reap a harvest if we do not give up." (Galatians 6:9)

THE HARDEST PART

Planting a seed beneath the soil
Does not require the greatest toil.
God sends down the rain and sun;
We don't control them—either one.

But weeds appear and multiply.
They spring up, tangled thick and high.
They choke the plant and kill the root.
They drink the moisture from the fruit.

Weeding tests the gardener's skill
It breaks his back and breaks his will
The garden's not too hard to start
But weeding—that's the hardest part!

Nancy Eichman

The people of Jesus' time were especially familiar with the arduous chore of weeding. These farmers battled many varieties of weeds, briars, thorns and thistles. Unlike today's agricultural techniques which use selected herbicides to control weeds, the ancient farmer had only one solution to the weed problem—clean cultivation of the soil. That was almost impossible with the wind and animals scattering seeds. Only with constant care could he gain any harvest at all.

So it is in keeping the soil of our spiritual garden clear of weeds. If we feel our garden needs no more work, we are vastly mistaken. The battle on evil wages on whether we enter the fray or not. This is illustrated in the parable of the tares (Matthew 13:24-30). While the farmer slept, the enemy sowed weeds in his garden.

114

So the devil is ready to sow the tares of evil in our hearts. The battle against evil is a constant one.

Scripture records one man who fought a battle against the enemies of the Lord on two fronts. His physical war was waged alone, without the help of another countryman or any army. His exploits of tremendous strength were told far and near. He killed the enemy by the thousands. He did all this because the "Spirit of the Lord" was upon him.

But his greatest struggle was an inward one against the lusts of the flesh. His death came as a result of his overwhelming desire for wine and women. His spiritual garden had begun well but the weeds of sin took over. Any good growth was choked with evil.

Let us look at the circumstances of Samson's mighty beginning and at the factors of his weakness and downfall.

"HOW TO" INSTRUCTIONS WITH SATISFACTION GUARANTEED?

Manoah and his wife were childless, but God had a special plan for them as parents. An angel appeared first to his wife and then again to both Manoah and his wife to announce the upcoming birth of a son.

Note Manoah's prayer in Judges 13:8: ". . .Oh Lord, I beg you, let the man of God you sent to us come again to teach us how to bring up the boy who is to be born." When the angel later appeared, Manoah asked, "When your words are fulfilled, what is to be the rule for the boy's life and work?"

Do you think Manoah had a case of first-time parent jitters? Perhaps. But I think his concern ran much deeper because he realized his great responsibility for bringing up this special child. Not only was his son to be "set apart to God from birth" by the Nazarite vow but he was destined to "begin the deliverance of Israel from the hands of the Philistines."

What if we had the same opportunity—to ask an angel for "how-to instructions" to bring up each particular child? Since every child is unique, we would need these instructions to be individualized and personal. We could use these as a guide in building the character of each child.

In a similar vein, how about a satisfaction guarantee that each child, no matter what their experience or heredity, would "turn out right." I am sure Manoah and his wife would have treasured such a guarantee.

But neither they nor we have that privilege. We have no set of instructions nor guarantees. We cannot sit back after we plant—we have to keep on teaching and training and weeding.

It seems Samson's parents were dedicated to their responsibility. No doubt Samson was diligently taught the Law but even more specifically his special calling and purpose. His Nazarite vow set him apart. Numbers 6:1-21 contains the three

115

Nazarite stipulations to which he was to adhere: (a.) no eating or drinking from a product of the vine, (b.) no contact with dead bodies, and (c.) his hair was not to be cut. (In manhood, the only regulation he continued to follow was keeping his hair uncut.)

WEED TROUBLE

The first recorded hint of "weed trouble" was Samson's desire for a Philistine wife. Not only did Samson disobey the law by seeking a foreign wife (Exodus 34:16; Deuteronomy 7:3) but he disregarded his father's authority by choosing his own wife. It was customary for the head of the family to choose the wife for his son. When Samson's parents urged him to consider one of the Israelite women, Samson curtly answered that the Philistine was "the right one for me." Manoah and his wife must have prayed fervently about this marriage and reluctantly allowed the ill-fated event.

But Samson did not learn from his experience with the Philistine woman (whom the Philistines burned along with her father). After visiting a prostitute in Gaza, where the Philistines lay in wait to kill him, he carried off the doors, doorposts and bar of the city gate for a distance of about 38 miles uphill!

Later he fell in love with Delilah and it was through the deceitful wiles of this Philistine woman that his downfall was imminent. After giving three false reasons for his strength, he disclosed the true key to his power. In his stupored sleep, he was betrayed to the enemy. They blinded him and gave him the menial task of grinding in the prison house.

Perhaps in his humbled position, Samson was able to think about his life. Perhaps here he became close to God—we do not know.

Finally, after asking God's help, Samson lost his life in the process of destroying an enemy temple where 3,000 Philistines had gathered to mock him. In this feat he killed more than he had in his lifetime.

WHAT WENT WRONG?

Was Samson's death justified? Was his life justified? Did his sacrificial death justify his riotous life—a life that was supposed to be committed as a Nazarite and as God's judge? Samson's strength was a graphic statement of God's power and blessing on a chosen vessel. Yet did he utilize that strength as effectively as he could? Was his parents' training sufficient? Was it their fault that Samson wandered after wine and women? Where did they go wrong? Where did he go wrong?

Though Samson lived thousands of years ago, the questions we ask about his life are relevant today. Parents wring their hands and ask, "Why has my child left the Lord?" How far does the blame go and where does it stop?

The Scriptures can help us understand these complex questions. We are not told much about Samson's earlier training but we know his parents cared about him, and the Lord blessed him. But as he reached manhood, he started making his own decisions and they were not wise ones. The tragic results of his bad judgement affected not only his own life but also the lives of others. He acted more like an uncontrollable juvenile delinquent than a judge of Israel. He was mighty in muscle but miniscule in mind. The weight of his problems rested squarely on his own shoulders (pun intended!). Whatever influence his parents played in his life, there came a time when he was his own man. Somehow, in his adult life, his spiritual garden was not weeded and spiritual things were choked out of his life.

Interestingly, Samson's name is on the roll of the Hall of Faith in Hebrews 11, along with Abraham, Moses and David. In all fairness, we must admit that all those listed were humans who failed at times. Samson did fulfill part of his purpose—to begin to deliver his people from the Philistines. But we wonder how much more he could have accomplished if he had exercised self-control in his life and had continued to follow God.

How can we guarantee our children will not fall away? Could all our teaching and training go down the tube?

The gardener can plant, water, fertilize and weed his garden but there is one thing he cannot do. He cannot MAKE a seed grow. He cannot force it to develop into a fruitful plant.

By the same token, we cannot force God's Word on our children and make it grow in their hearts. We might begin the process but it takes a willing heart to accept and obey its teachings. When a person reaches the age of accountability, he is responsible for his own actions. He can choose to do right or wrong. It is this freedom of choice that differentiates him from the animals. Every man is a free moral agent who can choose God or reject Him.

IS PROVERBS 22:6 A PROMISE?

But one might say, "What about the 'promise' in Proverbs 22:6. It states: 'Train a child in the way he should go, and when he is old he will not turn from it.' Isn't that a guarantee that if we train our children, they won't depart from God—at least for very long? Perhaps they might sow a little wild oats but nothing serious."

First, let us examine the context of this verse. This is a proverb or concise statement which is generally true but can have exceptions.

For example, Proverbs 3:1-2 states that if we keep God's commands, we will have prolonged lives and prosperity. Is this true in every case? Generally, godly people do live longer lives and insurance companies have proved this. But it is not ALWAYS true. How about Stephen or James or the countless other martyrs who lost their lives because they were Christians? What about fine Christians who die in the bloom of youth? And how many prosperous Christian millionaires do you know?

117

Likewise, in Proverbs 22:6 we see, not an unconditional guarantee, but rather a statement that is generally true. Across the board most children, conscientiously trained by their parents, will remain faithful to God. But there are exceptions.

LIKE FATHER, LIKE SON?

The Bible gives us many examples of godly parents whose children were evil. Look at the rebellious sons of Eli, Samuel, David and Solomon. The very writer of the previously mentioned proverb (22:6) raised Rehoboam, whose poor leadership divided the kingdom of Israel and led his country in idol worship.

Ezekiel 18:5-32 clearly teaches that a son can choose his own way. Verse 20 states, "The son who sins is the one who will die. The son will not share the guilt of the father, nor will the father share the guilt of the son. . ." If each child could blame his parents for his lost condition, then the buck would finally stop with Adam and Eve!

Ultimately, the choice to serve God lies within the heart of each responsible individual. It is a daily choice. No one can make it for someone else. On judgement day each person will stand alone (2 Corinthians 5:10).

DON'T GIVE UP

When godly parents have done all they can to train and teach their child, he still might not choose to follow God. With heavy hearts, they can pray and keep open lines of communication. And they should not give up hope on their offspring.

At the cemetery at Jamestown, Virginia, a tomb has been forced open by a tree that pushed its way through the stone. When it broke through, it was not the three feet diameter tree it is now. Rather it was a thriving sturdy sapling that slowly, day by day, pushed its way to the sunlight.

God's Word is like that, if given a chance. It is the "power of God unto salvation" and it can push through the hardest heart.

WHAT'S THE USE?

Knowing that we have no guarantees, we might doubt if our efforts are worthwhile. We can be assured, however, that continually teaching God's Word will not be useless.

> As the rain and the snow come down from heaven, and do not return to it without watering the earth and making it bud and flourish, so that it yields seed for the sower and bread for the eater, So is my word that goes out from my mouth: It will not return to me empty, but will accomplish what I desire and achieve the purpose for which I sent it (Isaiah 55:10-11).

> Therefore, my dear brothers, stand firm. Let nothing move you. Always give yourselves fully to the work of the Lord, because you know that your labor in the Lord is not vain (1 Corinthians 15:58).

As Samson's parents had no guarantees for a faithful child, so neither do we. We cannot know how our children will turn out. We can only try our best and trust God for the harvest. The wise man states: "Sow your seed in the morning, and at evening let not your hands be idle, for you do not know which will succeed, whether this or that, or whether both will do equally well" (Ecclesiastes 11:6). One thing is for sure—if we do not sow, we are sure to fail! Whether the soil brings forth fruit or weed, it's still up to us to plant the seed!

W. Phillip Keller shared the following poem in his book A GARDENER LOOKS AT THE FRUITS OF THE SPIRIT.

> My life is a garden.
> Your life is a garden.
> Is it a waste, untilled and wild?
> Like an untaught, untrained child?
> Or is it good soil under the Master's hand?
> Is my soul His own cherished land?
> Is it grown thick with thistles and weed?
> Or has it been sown with His good seed?
> What is the harvest that comes from this life?
> Goodness and love, or hatred and strife?
> O Lord, take this stony ground of mind.
> Make it all, completely Thine!
> Only then can it ever yield,
> The pleasant fruits of a godly field.

DON'T STOP NOW!

With the Israelites on the brink of Canaan and its idolatrous inhabitants, the Lord warned, "Only be careful, and watch yourselves closely so that you do not forget the things your eyes have seen or let them slip from your heart as long as you live. Teach them to your children and to their children after them" (Deuteronomy 4:9).

Note that parents were not to stop teaching when their children had become parents but rather were to teach their grandchildren too. Even grandmas and grandpas were not exempt from teaching! This teaching was passed on from generation to generation because of what they had seen the Lord do for them.

Interestingly, the only time "grandmother" is mentioned in the Bible is in reference to Eunice, Timothy's grandmother (2 Timothy 1:5). Here grandmother and mother Lois are praised for their godly influence on Timothy from infancy. But even with Timothy's tremendous biblical background, Paul encouraged him to keep working hard to correctly handle the word of truth (2 Timothy 2:15). Grandmother and mother helped plant the Seed but Timothy had to keep on learning and studying—and weeding.

Their illustrious example shows us how weeding must continue throughout the Christian life. Whether the Christian is seventeen or seventy, the weeding process cannot stop. Christians do not automatically stay faithful any more than a garden stays clear of weeds.

Someone has quipped, "Old gardeners never die. They just throw in the trowel!" Do we as parents spiritually throw in the trowel when our children graduate from high school? When they leave home? When they get married? Do we "retire" from teaching when we reach a certain age? When children are "out from under," a parent's influence is not quite the same but it can still be an effective power for good.

Susanna Wesley, the mother of religious leaders Samuel and Charles, knew the importance of weeding. She devoted an uninterrupted hour to each of her 19 children. That in itself is amazing, considering the demands of housework and growing children at that time. But even more incredible is that she invested that hour during the week in prayer after her children left home! She did not stop weeding.[1]

KEEPING THE WEEDS AWAY

It has been said, "A man of words and not of deeds is like a garden full of weeds." Keeping weeds from growing under our feet requires action. "...faith without deeds is dead" (James 2:26). Faith in action is the acid test of our Christianity. Repeatedly, we are reminded of this throughout the Bible. John, the apostle of love, wrote, "Dear childen, let us not love with words or tongue but with actions and in truth" (1 John 3:18). The wise man realized that laziness and inaction lead to ruin in our gardens and our lives as well. He wrote:

> I went past the field of the sluggard, past the vineyard of the man who lacks judgement; thorns had come up everywhere, the ground was covered with weeds, and the stone wall was in ruins. I applied my heart to what I observed and learned a lesson from what I saw: A little folding of the hands to rest—and poverty will come on you like a bandit and scarcity like an armed man (Ecclesiastes 24:30-34).

It is not always easy to keep on keeping on but with the Lord's help we can do it. Here are some ways to keep the weeds down and our enthusiasm up. These suggestions are not directed at any specific age since weeding goes on...and on...and on...

1. Find another Christian with whom you can discuss your personal Bible study. This may be especially meaningful to someone single, widowed or elderly.

2. Play tapes of Scripture, sermons and spiritual songs as you work.

3. Discover Christian encampments, camping vacations, singles' weekends, men's or women's retreats.

4. Teach or co-teach a class. Often the teacher learns more than the students.

5. Advertise Bible correspondence courses at a fair booth.

6. Initiate a neighborhood Bible study.

7. Distribute tracts and religious periodicals wherever they might be read—hospitals, offices, motels, airports.

8. Start a Bible hour or "Kids' Klub" for children in the church building or your home.

9. Test your knowledge with a Bible correspondence course.

10. Record worship services for the sick and shut-ins.

11. Support missionaries and college students away from home by an encouraging tape.

12. Listen to church-supported radio and TV programs.

DAILY RENEWAL

What keeps us going—day in and day out? What renews our spiritual souls? Paul answers, "Therefore we do not lose heart. Though outwardly we are wasting away, yet inwardly we are being renewed day by day" (2 Corinthians 4:16). What makes the weeding worth the sweat and toil? He goes on, "For our light and momentary troubles are achieving for us an eternal glory that far outweighs them all" (2 Corinthians 4:17). That is what makes the planning, preparing, planting, nurturing and weeding all worthwhile—the ETERNAL HARVEST!

CHAPTER 12
PULLING THE WEEDS
Digging Deeper

1. What were the three stipulations of the Nazarite vow?

2. In choosing a Philistine wife, how did Samson disregard his father and the Law?

3. Why do you think Samson was put in the "Hall of Faith" of Hebrews 11 with such spiritual giants as Abraham, Moses and David?

4. Is Proverbs 22:6 a guarantee for faithful children?

5. What Biblical examples of godly parents who had ungodly children can you think of?

6. Explain why Ezekiel 18:5-32 teaches personal accountability.

7. What responsiblity is given to parents whether their children remain faithful or not?

8. Where is the only time "grandmother" is mentioned in the Bible and in what context?

9. What is meant by the statement, "Faith has no grandchildren"?

10. How are Lois and Eunice good examples in weeding their spiritual gardens?

CHAPTER THIRTEEN

Reaping the Eternal Harvest

"Swing the sickle for the harvest is ripe. . ."
(Amos 3:13)

"Those who sow in tears will reap with songs of joy. He who goes out weeping, carrying seed to sow, will return with songs of joy, carrying sheaves with him."   *(Psalms 126:5-6)*

The gardener collapses into the nearest chair. The harvest has been gathered and put away. Every drop of sweat and hour of toil have been worthwhile. After all the planting, pruning, pickling, peeling, pitting, and packing, the results are evident. Lining the shelves are canning jars, brimming with produce in rainbow colors with myriad textures and shapes. The freezer boasts boxes of neatly labeled goods, ready for the year ahead. The bumper crop has yielded fresh leftovers for "just eatin'." The gardener reaches out his dirt-stained, calloused hand for an apple and eagerly sinks his teeth into the luscious ripe fruit that crunches with each juicy bite. He sighs and thanks the Lord for a plentiful harvest.

Probably none of us would toil in a garden if we could not visualize the eventual satisfaction of the scene above. Few things are quite as gratifying as eating produce that one has tenderly nurtured. And why not? Rewards in any area of life make work worth the trouble. Paul realized this fact in 2 Timothy 2:6: "The hardworking farmer should be the first to receive a share of the crops."

If we are faithful in the vineyard of God, we can anticipate a bountiful eternal harvest. Not only will our souls be eternally saved but also the souls of our families and others outside the family sphere.

There is a sense of completion in harvest—of fulfillment, of finishing a task to which one was once committed. There is an exhilaration in seeing a successfully completed mission. Let us look at one whose important purpose was fulfilled and what role his parents played in this task.

FULFILLING A PURPOSE

Few babies have been destined for such a role in history as Zechariah and Elizabeth's son! For a babe to be born to elderly parents was one thing—for those parents to bring forth the forerunner of the Messiah was quite another! This aged pair, belonging to the priestly tribe, had served God faithfully for years but they had no children.

Not every child's birth is foretold by an angel! In this case Gabriel delivered the birth-to-be announcement to an unbelieving father, administering to his priestly duties in the temple. Zechariah, "gripped with fear," asked for a sign and he got one! He could not speak until John was born.

Elizabeth was thrilled to be having this special baby but she also realized his secondary role to the Savior who would come. Upon Mary's visit to her home, Elizabeth exclaimed, "But why am I so favored, that the mother of my Lord should come to me? As soon as the sound of your greeting reached my ears, the baby in my womb leaped for joy" (Luke 1:43-44).

As John grew to maturity, Zechariah and Elizabeth must have prepared their son to fulfill the purpose God had for him. They took to heart what Gabriel had said about John,

> He will be a joy and delight to you, and many will rejoice because of his birth, for he will be great in the sight of the Lord. He is never to take wine or other fermented drink, and he will be filled with the Holy Spirit even from birth. Many of the people of Israel will he bring back to the Lord their God (Luke 1:14-16).

"A voice of one calling in the desert, Prepare the way for the Lord, make straight paths for him." So John is described by the prophet Isaiah. This so-named "Elijah" was a fulfillment of prophesy both in Isaiah and Malachi (Isaiah 40:3; Malachi 4:5-6). The key word to describe John's task lies in both these prophecies— PREPARE. John's mission was to prepare God's people for Christ.

No doubt John's parents had prepared him for the role he would play in relationship to the Messiah. John was aware that his own temporary popularity would be overshadowed by the glory of Christ. Christ was the Son, glowing ever more brightly; John would be a rising and falling star.

The Scriptures give us clues to John's devout and radical spirit. His habitat was the desert. His clothes—rough camel hair with a leather belt. His food— locusts and wild honey. This demonstrates the relative nonimportance luxury and convenience held in his life. The desert was a perfect place for man to pray, fast, and commune with God. (Remember where Jesus went several times to pray?)

When John took up the "fiery cloak of Elijah," he preached the baptism of repentance to the poor, Pharisees, tax collectors and soldiers. He rebuked king Herod himself because he was living with Herodias, his brother's wife. For his moral courage, John was cast into prison and eventually lost his head.

Before his death, however, John accomplished his task. It seems the people, even the unscrupulous tax collectors, accepted Jesus' words more easily when they had first been baptized by John. But the Pharisees and experts in the law rejected Jesus because they had not accepted John's message nor been baptized by him. John started preparing the soil of the people's hearts to accept the Seed but some soil was too hardened to receive it.

Jesus gave John a lasting tribute in Luke 7:28: "I tell you, among those born of women there is no greater than John; yet the one who is least in the kingdom of God is greater than he." What an honor was bestowed upon John. How much greater is our honor of being even the least in God's kingdom. John was great but he did not live long enough to become a member of Christ's church. What a privilege is ours to be Christians!

SPIRITUAL FARMER'S ALMANAC

Our spiritual harvest should begin at home with ourselves—and then our children. The Word gives us good advice about harvesting. It serves as a "Spiritual Farmer's Almanac" but its advice is never faulty, unclear, or based on conjecture. Let us look at what it says about reaping a spiritual harvest.

THE FARMER MUST BE PATIENT

A little girl and her dad were picking the red, vine-ripened tomatoes in their garden. She noticed the small green tomatoes on the vines and asked her dad, "Why don't we pick these?"

He answered, "Well, those are no good now."

After he went in, the child and her dog proceeded to destroy all the "no good" tomatoes!

That little girl had patience like some of us! We want patience and we want it NOW! But gardening instills patience like few other things do. After so much preparation, there comes a time to wait—and wait—and wait. James says, "See how the farmer waits for the land to yield its valuable crop and how patient he is for the autumn and spring rains. You too, be patient. . ." (James 5:7-8).

So it takes time for our spiritual harvest. Growth is a constant uphill progression. Maturity is a process of growth rather than a singular occurence. A plant breaking through the soil and unfolding in a few seconds is fascinating to watch in time-lapsed photography, but it just does not happen that way.

125

In our eagerness for our children to become Christians, it might be easy to push a little (or a lot). Encouraging is one thing and forcing is another. We need to know the difference! Otherwise, a child that is forced to obey the gospel will later wonder why he did it—to please the Lord or his parents. It might take longer than we think it should but is it not better to let the child make his own decision? Patience and time allow invisible seed to produce visible results. Just as we do not always understand how a seed grows under the ground so we do not always comprehend how God's Word can work in a human heart. It takes time for a seed to germinate under the soil with the right combination of heat, water and nutrients. Even when the first visible green shoot appears, growth continues until the harvest. Jesus illustrated gradual Christian maturity of the spiritual seed in the soil of the heart by this parable:

> ...A man scatters seed on the ground. Night and day, whether he sleeps or gets up, the seed sprouts and grows, though he does not know how. All by itself the soil produces grain—first the stalk, then the head, then the full kernel in the head. As soon as the grain is ripe, he puts the sickle to it, because the harvest has come (Mark 4:26-29).

Baptism marks not the end result but rather a fresh beginning to a new life of growth. The harvest does not end with a person becoming a Christian but continues until the Great Reaper returns. Our lives and our children's lives should be constantly maturing. Peter urged, "But grow in the grace and knowledge of our Lord and Savior Jesus Christ" (2 Peter 3:18).

Patience does not come easily for us. Ours is an instant world—instant mixes, fast food, speedy deliveries, jiffy printers, quick money, mad dashes, accelerated speeds, express carriers and even brisk tea! But there is no such thing as instant spiritual growth. That only comes from continual study of God's Word and application of that Word.

A younger man, who greatly revered an elderly preacher for his scholarship and maturity, once asked him, "How did you become such a Bible scholar?" The older man replied, "I studied the Word every day for 50 years!" The old hair cream commercials boast of "a little dab 'll do ya" does not work when it comes to Christian growth. Let us be patient with ourselves and our children—and the growth in Christ that hopefully will come. As the saying goes, "Be patient with me—God isn't finished with me yet."

BUT THE HARVEST CANNOT WAIT

The farmer's patience for the harvest need not last forever. The time comes when that patience turns to the urgency of the harvest. If the farm is a large one, more equipment will be needed. Extra workers might be hired. Workdays are extended. The farmer's future prosperity might hang upon the moment. The crops are ready—they must be harvested now!

As a plant matures, it eventually reaches the peak of its blossom, texture and, if edible, taste. If harvested before its time, it would still be "green" and tough. If harvested after its peak, at best it might be mushy; at worst, it could be downright rotten! So it is best that every farmer picks his harvest at its peak, that time when everything is right and ready.

There is a time when our children will hopefully be right and ready for baptism and a future life of service to God. If we have tried to sow the Word in their hearts, we will hopefully be responsive to that time. If they are urged to wait, they may lose interest in spiritual things altogether. It is up to us to be aware when they are ready and encourage them to obey Christ. If it takes walking down the aisle with them or calling the preacher at midnight or baptizing them ourselves, whatever—let US be ready when they are ready.

Jesus warned His disciples to perceive the immediate need for spiritually harvesting. "Do you not say, 'Four months more and then the harvest'? I tell you, open your eyes and look at the fields! They are ripe for harvest" (John 4:35).

If we neglect the urgency of harvest, the opportunity will be lost. How tragic if at judgement our children were to cry to us: "The harvest is past, the summer has ended, and we are not saved" (Jeremiah 8:20).

WE WILL REAP WHAT WE SOW

One thing is certain—if the farmer plants green beans, he will NOT reap cabbage! From creation, God made plants to reproduce after their own kind. The product of our harvest depends on what we plant.

Also, the extent of our harvest depends on the intensity of our efforts prior to the harvest. If the gardener takes the time to lovingly prepare and cultivate his garden, the harvest will be plentiful indeed. If the gardener puts in a half-hearted effort, the garden will fail to produce its potential.

What is true in nature is also applicable to our spiritual life. Paul tells the Corinthians: "Remember this: whoever sows sparingly will also reap sparingly, and whoever sows generously will also reap generously" (2 Corinthians 9:6). He also warned the Galatians: "Do not be deceived: God cannot be mocked. A man reaps what he sows. The one who sows to please his sinful nature, from that nature will reap destruction, the one who sows to please the Spirit, from the Spirit will reap eternal life" (Galatians 6:7-8).

His meaning is obvious. If we practice God's will in our lives and instill His Words in our children's hearts, a harvest of goodness will be brought forth. If His Words mean nothing to us or our children, the harvest will be pretty skimpy spiritually.

Hosea urged the nation of Israel to:

Sow for yourselves righteousness, reap the fruit of unfailing love, and break up your unplowed ground; for it is time to seek the Lord, until he comes and showers righteousness on you. But you have planted wickedness, you have reaped evil, you have eaten the fruit of deception. Because you have depended on your own strength. . ." (Hosea 10:12-13).

We cannot escape God's Law of nature. If we are committed to put God first in teaching our children, then the results will show!

ONE MAY HARVEST WHAT ANOTHER HAS SOWN

One definitely reaps the product of WHAT he sows, but at times someone other than the sower might do the reaping. If we sow good things in our children's hearts, another might reap the fruition of their obedience to the gospel. That is O.K. Even our Lord harvested where Moses, the prophets, and John the Baptist had sown in preparation for His coming. Through their preparation even the adulterous woman at the well was aware that a Messiah was coming who would explain everything to them. By her testimony many Samaritans believed in Christ and more believed after they heard Jesus' words.

It was in this context that Jesus told His disciples,

Even now the reaper draws his wages, even now he harvests the crop for eternal life, so that the sower and the reaper may be glad together. Thus the saying, 'One sows and another reaps' is true. I sent you to reap what you have not worked for. Others have done the hard work, and you have reaped the benefits of their labor (John 4:36-38).

Through the preparation of others, the Samaritans were ready for a spiritual awakening. Then the Lord and His disciples were able to reap the harvest.

It is the crowning joy of a Christian father to baptize his son or daughter into Christ. It is no insult to him, however, if another does the baptizing. Praise God for the harvest—whoever reaps or sows!

ONE MUST BEAR A QUANTITY AND QUALITY OF FRUIT

Bearing fruit is what the harvest is really all about. Jesus is interested in His servants bearing "fruit that will last eternally" (John 15:16). We have a literal illustration of how Jesus felt about fruitless plants in Matthew 21:18-21. Jesus, feeling the pangs of hunger, reached up to pluck a fig from a fig tree at its peak. Upon finding no edible fruit, Jesus cursed the tree. It should have been laden with fruit but it boasted only leaves. This demonstrates God's displeasure with those who are leaved-out spiritually but produce no fruit.

One ripe luscious fig would have meant so much to our hungry Lord. Likewise spiritually one soul is precious to Him. The parables of the Lost Sheep and the

Lost Coin demonstrate to us the value of one soul (Luke 15:4-7). The importance of the single soul is evident in Jesus' daily encounters with people as He walked the dusty roads of Palestine.

But would Jesus have been satisfied with only one fig from a tree capable of producing many more? I do not believe so. He expects a quantity of harvest, proportional with the fruit-bearing capacity of the plant. So it is with our spiritual capabilities. The parable of the talents demonstrates that the Lord is not critical of the five talent man who does the best he can, even though he does not produce as much as the ten talent man. Rather the one talent man is condemned because he does nothing to produce any fruit at all.

In John 15:8 we learn Christ expects us to "bear much fruit." Note he did not say just to "bear fruit" or "bear some fruit." In fact, "bearing much fruit" serves as a proof of our discipleship.

However, quantity of harvest is not all the Lord cares about. He is concerned about quality. Warning of the bad fruit of false teachers, he explains:

By their fruit you will recognize them. Do people pick grapes from thornbushes, or figs from thistles? Likewise every good tree bears good fruit, but a bad tree bears bad fruit. A good tree cannot bear bad fruit, and a bad tree cannot bear good fruit. Every tree that does not bear good fruit is cut down and thrown into the fire. Thus, by their fruit you will recognize them (Matthew 16-20).

The famous agriculturalist Luther Burbank once said, "I am trying to make every flower that grows in my garden produce as full a blossom as possible."[1] So should be the quality in our spiritual garden. It is interesting to note that in Galatians 5, Paul speaks of the FRUIT and not the FRUITS of the Spirit. Perhaps his list of nine specific traits combine to make up the total facet of a mature Christian character just like the petals of a rose.

It is clear that the Lord requires quality fruit from His followers. It is also plain what will happen to those who do not produce good fruit.

The ax is already at the root of the trees, and every tree that does not produce good fruit will be cut down and thrown into the fire. . .His winnowing fork is in his hand, and he will clear his threshing floor, gathering the wheat into his barn and burning up the chaff with unquenchable fire" (Matthew 3:10,12).

So we can see that the Lord expects a bifold dimension in our harvest—quantity and quality.

BEYOND OUR WALLS?

We have stressed "family first" in teaching God's Word. Does this sound like "Lord, bless us four and no more"? Is the spiritual fruit produced in our family to overflow no further than our house's walls?

A resounding "NO!" Our harvest begins in our families but it does not stop there. Perhaps our family could be compared to a fortress. Before a commander can take the offensive and charge against the enemy, he must make sure his fortress is secure. Ammunition needs to be gathered, sentries posted, and food stored for any impending attack. Then if he needs to retreat, he will be well-prepared for battle or siege. A commander would be foolish to leave his fortress unprotected. But he also would be foolish if he always stayed inside the fortress just waiting for attack.

So it is with or families. We can prepare and fortify our children against the enemy, the devil. With the Lord's help, together what a united front we can have! But if we remain always inside the fortress, what good is our preparation? And must we not be on the offensive outside the shelter of our homes "to quench all the fiery darts of the wicked." No wonder the Christian is compared to a soldier with armour, breastplate, shield and helmet! (Ephesians 6:10-18).

It may be that some families are letting their spiritual weapons rust from lack of use. As they comfortably sit, munching their cornchips and watching TV in their toasty homes, millions out in the cold, dark world long for the warmth of Christ. Sharing Christ is what the Good News is all about and the sharing goes beyond our families.

Our children need to see us sharing the Good News with our friends and our neighbors. It will then seem more natural for them to talk to their friends about Jesus. We need to take the Great Commission seriously so they will too.

FULFILLING THE MISSION

John the Baptist was fulfilling his purpose by sharing the message. So should we. But his specific life purpose was to preach and prepare for the Messiah. Am I saying we all need to begin proclaiming the Word in the desert? Does that mean we need to start donning camel hair, accented with leather belts? Locust and wild honey, anyone?

No, John's specific purpose was not ours. But we all have the God-given responsibility to share the Good News that has been shared with us. If John were to sit content in his knowledge of who Jesus was without sharing it, it would be like sitting on a time bomb ready to explode. His message would not wait. Neither can ours!

The Lord could look out and see the need for more harvesters for the millions who needed Him. He told His disciples, "The harvest is plentiful but the workers are few. Ask the Lord of the harvest, therefore, to send out workers into his harvest field" (Matthew 9:37).

MORE THAN BEFORE

The miracle of the seed is its reproductive quality. Seed has been the reproductive vehicle of most living things from the beginning of time. So it is not surprising that Christ used the seed analogy to show how Christians can "reproduce" other Christians. Not only should the Lord's people bring forth the "fruit of the Spirit" (Galatians 5) but they should also propagate more believers. Else how will the species of a plant (or the church) survive to the next generation? Our goal is "more than before."

Paul spoke of the propagating power of the gospel in Colossians 1:6. "...All over the world this gospel is producing fruit and growing, just as it has been doing among you since the day you heard it and understood God's grace in all its truth." The apostle commended the Colossians for their faith and love and prayed that they "...may live a life worthy of the Lord and may please him in every way: bearing fruit in every good work, growing in the knowledge of God..." (Colossians 1:10).

Sometimes we limit the harvest and fruit-bearing ability of the gospel with our myopic view of our families and the church. Consider this parable, told by Neil Thannisch.

THE PARABLE OF THE ORANGE GROVES

I was driving down a long Florida highway that was lined on both sides by wide expanses of orange groves. The boughs of all the trees were bent by the ripening fruit. There were no other cars on the road with me and nobody in sight harvesting the abundant crop of oranges.

After driving further, I came upon a sign that read "LEAVING GROVES COUNTY" and another sign that read "ENTERING HOME COUNTY." The density of the orange trees dropped at the county line and there was a building built around each of what few trees there were. Suddenly I was surrounded by a large throng of people moving through the streets. Enjoying the change of pace, I parked the car to walk around and watch the people. I figured I had reached the town during some sort of interesting celebration. I noticed how all of the nicely dressed people were talking and laughing and strolling the streets with evidently several different destinations. Upon closer observation, I also noticed that most carried nice leather books entitled ORANGE PICKER'S MANUAL engraved in gold on the cover.

Curious, I asked the closest passer-by the meaning of all this. She looked at me rather strangely for a moment and then smiling, she replied, "You must be new here. You see, once a year we must take time out of our busy schedules to study our ORANGE PICKER'S MANUAL so that we can become better orange pickers." The woman left me standing there while she went to join her friends.

Still curious, I followed another group of people into one of the buildings that surrounded a large orange tree. Trying to look like I knew what I was doing, I took a seat next to an older gentleman. All at once everything in the building went quiet and all the smiles quickly vanished from every face in the room except for a slim man at the front of the room. I was furnished a book entitled GREAT SONGS OF THE ORANGE GROVES. While the smiling slim man at the front frantically waved his arms, we sang several different songs. I turned to the gentleman beside me and asked, "When do we start picking oranges?"

He smiled and replied, "Very soon, just be patient."

I looked around and noticed that in the other buildings around the other trees the same thing was happening. Next, a big overweight man with rosy cheeks stood and started speaking about the big crop of oranges that needed to be picked. On and on he talked. I woke up when he started screaming and pointing around at the other buildings. But in the other buildings the men up front were screaming and pointing at our building. I knew the big man had reached the climax of his speech when his face turned bright red. Then, for a man of his size, he moved quickly to the tree and shook it with all his might and two oranges fell from the tree and landed in the baskets below. The applause was deafening. "Now do we start picking?" I asked the man beside me.

"What do you think we've been doing?" he cried. Astonished, I turned and walked back to my car.

I left town and drove back into GROVES COUNTY. Except for one or two harvesters against the horizon, there was no one to be seen. As I drove, the oranges on the trees began to fall to the ground and quickly rot. The earth shook violently as a voice echoed, "Pray to the Lord of harvest that He may send forth reapers."

We need to see the harvest beyond Home County. Our children need to perceive that a lost world means lost souls in every place all over the globe. How can we give our children this worldwide view of missions that encompasses not only across the street but across the ocean? Here are some suggestions to begin.

1. Buy a globe or wall map to make family members aware of the size of the world in relation to their home. (Even New York City looks tiny compared to the world!)

2. Find out which countries have few or no Christians. Try to discover why—climate? government? distance? How could these obstacles be overcome?

3. If a certain country appeals to your child, let him research its religions, customs and dress.

4. Write to missionaries to discover their particular needs and wants.

5. Correspond with pen pals (perhaps with ages near those of your children) which could be obtained from missionaries. Besides encouraging both their child and yours, it provides an outlet for expressing the joys and frustrations of mission work.

6. Purchase small items to fill a "WE CARE" package for missionaries.

7. Send missionaries one outgrown outfit or toy and one new one to stress sharing.

8. Make it possible for your child to participate in door-knocking and campaigning.

9. Invite current or retired missionaries to share their experiences in your home and congregation.

10. Encourage your child to dedicate his life to mission work.

Every child born gives parents another opportunity to carry out the Great Commission. The message of the Good News is much like the ripples made by a pebble thrown in a still pond. The waves begin at the point at which the rock hits the water but they soon radiate to the outer edges of the pond. So should the message radiate from its starting point—the home—and spread to the outer reaches of the globe.

Our children are one of our most precious possessions. We are abhorred at any parent who would mistreat his child. We gasp at the ogre who would place his child's hand in a fire or withhold water from him or lock him in a closet. We cannot conceive how anyone could do such a thing.

Yet some parents, by their spiritual neglect, are doing nothing to prevent their children from spending eternity where no light pierces the darkness, no water quenches thirst, and no cooling comfort exists from the unextinguishable heat. Truly hell is an agony we all want to miss. Never would we want our children there. Yet what are we doing to avoid it?

Can you imagine the double horror of burning in the flames of hell and there, through the smoke, seeing our suffering child in the next flame. What a terrible picture!

On the other hand, picture the ecstasy of heaven—the joy and serenity of peace with God in eternity—and seeing your child there too. THAT is worth working for!

RAISED AT HOME

The marvels of modern rapid transit is ever impressive. Fruits and vegetables on your dinner table could have been picked thousands of miles away a few days before. However, something is lost in the tradeoff. The ripe texture is lost to a firmer one that withstands the bumps and spills of the journey. The color of naturally ripened fruit is sacrificed for speed. After the harvest has been picked, packed and pummeled across country, the tangy tartness or tantalizing sweetness is gone. Technology can do many things but it cannot beat the taste of a homegrown fruit or vegetable, freshly picked from one's own garden.

Undoubtedly, "raised at home" is best.

Is that not true with our family's spiritual growth? The church can teach them. The Christian school can greatly aid in the training process. But "raised at home" is best. Parents are given the primary responsibility of preparing and tending their children's hearts for God. Will we fulfill that responsibility or ship them across town or cross-country for someone else to do our job?

Personal responsibility to "raise at home" was important to the ultimate goal of victory in the United States in the last days of World War II. The country faced critical food shortages due to the lend-lease agreements and relief programs that sent food to American soldiers and war-ravaged victims in Europe and the Pacific. With complete victory not far away, President Harry Truman called on everyone from children to the elderly to tend "victory gardens." He encouraged each family to start a bigger and better garden wherever they could—back yard, farm acreage, or community plot—and to see it through to harvest.

The ultimate goal of a greater victory looms on our spiritual horizon and we are each called to do what we can. How are OUR "victory gardens" faring? Will our harvest be a crop failure or a record bumper crop? With victory almost in sight but not in hand, do we grow faint? We are told in 1 Corinthians 15:57, "But thanks be to God! He gives us the victory through our Lord Jesus Christ." And what an eternal victory that will be!

"Now he who supplies seed to the sower and bread for food will also supply and increase your store of seed and will enlarge the harvest of your righteousness" (1 Corinthians 9:10). Lord, help us meet the challenge of the harvest. The lost world beckons. The fields are ripe for harvest. But help us first harvest in our own homes. Help us to tend our own gardens first.

CHAPTER 13
REAPING THE ETERNAL HARVEST
Digging Deeper

1. Who was described as another "Elijah" and why?

2. Why do you think Zechariah and Elizabeth had taught their son his secondary role to the Savior?

3. What one word describes John the Baptist's purpose in life?

4. Using Jesus' illustration in Mark 4:26-29, explain how spiritual growth in the heart is like the gradual growth from a seed.

5. Why is patience imperative in waiting for the spiritual harvest?

6. In what context did Jesus speak of the urgency of the harvest in John 4:35?

7. How had Moses, the prophets, and John the Baptist prepared the people for Christ's coming?

8. In John 15:8 what serves as a proof of our discipleship?

9. Explain how the Lord expects quality as well as quantity in our spiritual harvest.

10. How do you feel we can give our children a more worldwide view of missions?

NOTES

HOW DOES YOUR GARDEN GROW
1. Joyce Hardin, "Helping Children Develop Their Own Faith," **Christian Woman,** July-August 1986, pp. 53-54.

BUT I DON'T HAVE A GREEN THUMB!
1. John Holt, **Teach Your Own** (New York: Delecorte Press/Seymour Lawrence, 1981), p. 51.
2. Mary White, **Growing Together** (Colorado Springs, CO: NAVPRESS, 1981), p. 16.
3. Guy N. Woods, **James** (Nashville: Gospel Advocate Co., 1964), p. 83.
4. Quoted by Laurence J. Peter, **Peter's Quotations—Ideas for Our Time** (New York: William Morrow and Company, Inc., 1977), p. 103.
5. Kitty D. Weaver, **Lenin's Grandchildren** (New York: Simon and Schuster, 1971), p. 97.
6. Quoted by Elton Trueblood and Pauline Trueblood, **The Recovery of Family Life** (New York: Harper and Row, 1953), p. 20.

PLANNING THE GARDEN
1. Gretchen Hirsch, **WOMANHOURS: A 21-Day Time Management Plan That Works** (New York: St. Martin's Press, 1983), p. 39.
2. Quoted by Linda Howard, **Mothers Are People Too** (Plainfield, NJ: Logos International, 1976), p. 13.
3. Quoted by Mary Oler, "I have Time!" **1983 Harding University Lectures** (Delight, AR: Gospel Light Publishing Company, 1983), p. 133.
4. Doug Parsons, "Day by Day With God," **1977 Harding University Lectures** (Austin, TX: Firm Foundation, 1977), p. 301.
5. **The Bible Commentary (Proverbs-Ezekiel)** ed. F.C. Cook (Grand Rapids, MI: Baker Book House, 1981), p. 62.
6. June Crabtree, **Teach 'Em Like God Made 'Em** (Cincinnati, OH: Standard Publishing Company, 1976), p. 47.
7. Charles Swindoll, **You and Your Child** (Nashville: Thomas Nelson Inc., 1977), p. 66.
8. John Kachelman, "Parents 'Have You Considered My Servant Job?'" **Christian Bible Teacher,** October 1985, pp. 437-438.

GATHERING THE TOOLS
1. Dick Van Dyke, **Faith, Hope and Hilarity** (Garden City, N.Y.: Doubleday, 1970), p. 16.

A LITTLE HELP FROM OUR FRIENDS
1. Jane McWhorter, "The Power of the Seed," **Christian Bible Teacher,** February 1986, p. 61.

THE EVER VIABLE SEED

1. Neale Pryor, **You Can Trust Your Bible** (Abilene, TX: Quality Publications, 1980), p. 15-16.
2. Quoted by F. Furman Kearley, "My Precious Bible Book Divine—Part I," **Christian Bible Teacher,** January 1986, p. 7.
3. Pryor, p. 16.
4. Jack P. Lewis, **The English Bible From KJV to NIV—A History and Evaluation** (Grand Rapids, MI: Baker Book House, 1984), pp. 20-24.
5. Pryor, p. 17.
6. F. Furman Kearley, "My Precious Bible Book Divine—Part II," **Christian Bible Teacher,** February 1986, p. 56.
7. J. Lewis, pp. 13-16, 18.
8. Annie May Lewis, "Give Me the Bible," **Christian Woman,** January-February 1987, pp. 15, 19.
9. Gordon D. Fee and Douglas Stuart, **How to Read the Bible for All Its Worth** (Grand Rapids, MI: Zondervan Publishing House, 1982), p. 31.
10. Warren Wiersbe, **Do It! Creative Bible Studies for Youth** (Tempe, AZ: Success With Youth Publications, Inc., 1973), pp. 72-73.
11. **How to Study the Bible,** ed. John B. Job (Downers Grove, IL: Inter Varsity Press, 1979), p. 13.
12. **How to Study the Bible,** pp. 26-27.
13. Arthur Maxwell, **Your Bible and You** (Washington, D.C.: Review and Herald Publishing Association, 1959), pp. 22-23.
14. Tim LaHaye, **How To Study the Bible for Yourself** Eugene, OR: Harvest House, 1976), p. 128.

A TIME TO SOW

1. Rossel, Seymour, **Judaism** (New York: Franklin Watts, Inc., 1976), pp. 47-48, 50.
2. Quoted by F. Furman Kearley, "Building Dynamic Churches Through Dynamic Bible Schools," **Gospel Advocate,** September 4, 1986, p. 518.
3. White, p. 12.
4. Quoted by Kay Kuzma, **Working Mothers** (Los Angeles: Stratford Press, 1981), pp. 13-14.
5. Wayne Rickerson, **Family Fun and Togetherness** (Wheaton, IL: Victor Books, 1979), p. 43.

PREPARING THE SOIL

1. White, pp. 88-90.
2. Gene Stallings, "Performance is Topic of Stallings," **Searcy Citizen,** February 27, 1987, p. 1.
3. Swindoll, pp. 18-21, 65.
4. Marian M. Schoolland, **Leading Little Ones To God** (Grand Rapids, MI:

William B. Eerdmans, 1962), p. viii.
5. Quoted by Jim Trelease, **The Read Aloud Handbook** (New York: Penguin Books, 1985) p. 43.
6. Cindy LeBlanc, "The Worship Bag," **Christian Bible Teacher,** December 1985, pp. 514-515.
7. Judy Miller, **Seasons of the Heart** (Nashville: Gospel Advocate Co., 1984) p. 60.

PLANTING THE SEED
1. Janis Dearman, "The Three R's of Spiritual Education," **Christian Bible Teacher,** January 1987, p. 32.
2. Peggy Eastman and John L. Barr, **Your Child Is Smarter Than You Think** (New York: William Morrow and Company, Inc., 1985), p. 43.
3. Paul D. Meier, **Christian Child-Rearing and Personality Development** (Grand Rapids, MI: Baker Book House, 1977), p. ix.
4. Wynelle F. Main, "Stages of Childhood Development—Part IV—Honesty," **Christian Bible Teacher,** January 1986, p. 25.
5. Wynelle F. Main, "Stages of Childhood Development—Part V—How Does Memory Grow?" **Christian Bible Teacher,** February 1986, p. 68-69.
6. For more details see: Kay Kuzma, **Teaching Your Own Preschool Children** (Garden City, N.Y.: Doubleday and Co., Inc., 1980), pp. 157-160.
7. Joyce Milburn, **Helping Your Children Love Each Other** (Minneapolis, MN: Bethany House Publishers, 1983), p. 82.

NURTURING THE SOIL
1. White, pp. 96-102.

WATERING JUST RIGHT
1. James I. Packer, **The Bible Almanac** (Nashville: Thomas Nelson Publishers, 1980), p. 453.
2. Eleanor Doan, **Teaching Junior Highs Successfully** (Glendale, CA: Gospel Light Publications, 1962), p. 6.
3. Benny B. Bristow, "What are Teenagers Like?" **Christian Bible Teacher,** October 1985, pp. 428-429.

PULLING THE WEEDS
1. Swindoll, p. 154.

REAPING THE ETERNAL HARVEST
1. Quoted by Peter Ainslie, **Cultivating the Fruit of the Spirit** (St. Louis: Bethany Press, 1968), p. 19.